# THE STORY OF THE LOCH NESS MONSTER

**A TARGET MYSTERY**

# THE STORY OF THE LOCH NESS MONSTER

## TIM DINSDALE

*a division of*
Universal-Tandem Publishing Co., Ltd.
14 Gloucester Road, London SW7 4RD

First published simultaneously in Great Britain
by Allan Wingate (Publishers) Ltd.,
and Universal-Tandem Publishing Co., Ltd., 1973

Second impression, 1973

ISBN 0 426 10073 5

Printed in Great Britain by The Anchor Press Ltd.,
and bound by Wm. Brendon & Son Ltd., both of Tiptree, Essex

To my friends—
The Monster-hunters

# Acknowledgements

I would like to thank those who have contributed towards the writing of this book by providing me with information and in some cases their eye-witness accounts. In particular, Mr. Alexander Campbell, Mr. E. A. Aldridge, Mrs. Kay Shakespeare, Mrs. E. Essex, and Mrs. Elizabeth Montgomery Campbell of the Loch Morar Survey Committee.

I am indebted to the following copyright holders for permission to reproduce photographs . . . Plate 1, Associated Newspapers, Ltd; Plate 2, Mr. P. A. Mac-Nab; Plate 3, Camera Press, Ltd; Plate 4, Mr. R. H. Lowrie; Plates 7 & 8, The Academy of Applied Science and the Loch Ness Investigation Bureau, Ltd. I am particularly indebted, along with my publishers, to Messers. Routledge and Kegan Paul, Ltd., for permission to reproduce the following drawings from their book *Loch Ness Monster* . . . Figs. 1, 4, 5, 6, 8 and 9.

To all those other Monster-hunters whose names I remember but which are too numerous to mention I can only say 'thank you for your company, good cheer and moral support in both the good times and the bad.'

T.D.

# Contents

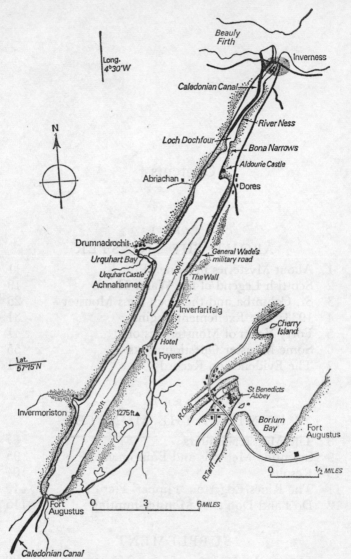

Figure 1 Map of Loch Ness

8

# Part I

# ABOUT THE MONSTER

# I

# About Mysteries in General

Most people, and this includes young people as well as adults, are fascinated by mysteries. In a world where we are surrounded by machines, and motor-cars, and everyday things like schools and shops and television, we get used to our lives running like clockwork, in an orderly 'tick-tock' sort of way. This, of course, makes life easier for everyone, but at the same time it can become a little dull.

That is probably why most people are curious, too—they like to enquire into matters which are not properly understood, over which there hangs an atmosphere of mystery. In a game of hide-and-seek, we like to peer around corners, to look into the unknown. Sometimes this can cause us to be surprised, or even become a bit anxious on occasion, but it does help to make the game exciting.

There are two kinds of mystery. There are mysteries which are entirely real—events which have happened but which cannot be explained, and there are mysteries which have grown out of the stories people tell about them, but which cannot be proven.

Of the first kind of mystery, perhaps one of the best

examples can be found in the case of the famous deserted sailing-ship, the *Mary Celeste*. This ship was discovered sailing through the ocean with no one on board, although she had left her home port with a normal crew, and passengers.

What happened to make everyone suddenly abandon ship will always remain a mystery. Some think there may have been a series of accidents with people falling overboard, and others diving in to help them, with the last of the crew putting out in the ship's boat in a desperate rescue attempt, only to be left behind by the unmanned *Mary Celeste*. Others believe the crew to have been poisoned by food, and driven temporarily mad, to jump overboard into the sea. Still others suggest that the crew was pulled over the side by the tentacles of a giant squid, which has been known to attack quite large sailing vessels!

The mystery of the *Mary Celeste* is real, and although books and articles have been written on the subject no one will ever be able to solve the riddle.

Of the second kind of mystery, ghosts is an example. People claim to have seen them, but no one has ever been able to measure a ghost with a tape-measure! It would be very difficult for anyone to *prove* a ghost, but we enjoy hearing stories about them.

Another good example of the more unreal—the 'is it or isn't it?' type of mystery is very up-to-date, and most people in most countries have heard about it, too. This mystery is caused by reports of 'Flying Saucers'. With so many different people claiming to have seen strange objects in the sky, which do not appear to be ordinary aircraft, and which behave in a very odd manner, it is not surprising that governments take an interest in them. But again, unfortunately, as far as we know no one has been able to catch one, or force one to land, or do more than take very blurred pictures of a flying saucer; and in consequence a great many people are not convinced they are real, though they are probably as interested by the mystery they represent, as you or I.

There are some mysteries which have already been proved to be false, and which originally must have grown out of tall stories told by someone years ago. An example is the 'Indian Rope Trick'. In this, a rope is said to writhe out of a wicker-basket like a snake, to the wail of an Indian snake-charmer's pipe. A small Indian boy assistant then climbs up the rope, and *disappears*. Of course, this is nonsense and no-one has ever seen the rope-trick performed although they might claim they knew of someone else who had. Some years ago I asked an Indian friend of mine if he had ever seen the trick himself, and he replied 'no'. He said he did not know what I was talking about, and had never heard of the 'Indian Rope Trick'. This convinced me the whole thing was an invention.

Native customs, however, sometimes involve true mysteries which appear to defy the laws of physics as we understand them. 'Fire-walking' is an example, in which the native dancers or worshippers seem able to walk across a pit filled with white-hot stones, without suffering burns or injury. Of course, people who go without shoes develop thick layers of skin on the soles of their feet, but this does not explain the fire-walking mystery. Whatever their secret may be, which enables them to perform this ritual, we of the western world are ignorant of it, and we would be foolish to try and copy what they do.

In natural-history, there are some amazing mysteries which in our present state of knowledge we are unable to explain. Perhaps one day soon, scientists will find out how it is that homing-pigeons can fly a direct route back to their lofts, when they have been sent hundreds of miles away in railway trains cooped up in baskets. Quite obviously they cannot see where they are going, and yet they get home by the shortest route once they are let out of the basket.

Fish, too, can behave in a manner which is mysterious. Baby salmon develop from eggs laid and fertilised by their parents in streams and rivers. Later these small fish travel down river to the sea where they disappear into deep water. For several years they live in the oceans slowly gaining weight, swimming hundreds and thousands of miles during this period of time. When they become adult they in their turn feel the urge to travel back to the rivers of their birth, to lay eggs, or spawn. The strange thing is that these fish make their way back without the use of compasses, or radio, or the maths and instruments we humans use to navigate. And yet, except for accidents like being eaten by seals or other bigger fish on the way homewards, they find their way back to the rivers and pools where they hatched out from the eggs. We cannot explain this either. It is another natural mystery.

Probably the best examples of mysteries that are now understood can be found in science, and chemistry in particular. Chemistry sets are sold in the shops, and experiments can be made at home changing the colour of fluids, and causing other strange reactions. At school a chemistry teacher is able to perform tricks with different materials which produce altogether magical effects. The changes come about because of known chemical reactions, but centuries ago these changes *were* thought to be magical, and the experimenters, or 'alchemists' as they were known, were sometimes asked to change lead, or tin, or some other inexpensive metal, into gold. Kings and queens in the past have been interested in doing this, hoping to become rich, but of course none of the alchemists was able to make gold in this way, though most of them tried, and some even pretended that they had found the secret.

Another great natural mystery is the human brain. The best doctors and surgeons of today are the first to admit that they don't know how it works, although they know a great deal about the parts of the brain, and about what it can accomplish. Of all the human organs it is by far the most remarkable, but the day may come when we are able to find the key to its overall performance.

Another extraordinary mystery which it is thought has to do with the human brain is hypnotism—the power to influence the brains of other people through suggestion, by *willing* them to do things, or to behave in a manner which is not of their own choice. Until a few years ago hypnotists were allowed to perform on stage, and it would be a common sight for a dozen or so people from the audience who had volunteered to work as guinea-pigs, to be seen laughing or crying or dancing about foolishly in response to the commands of the hypnotist who had put them under the influence of his own brain, or perhaps the power of his thoughts. We don't know how hypnotism works, or 'mesmerism' as it is sometimes called after a man named Mesmer who was the first to experiment seriously with hypnotism about a hundred years ago. It took a long time for his work to be recognised, but today it is, and hypnotism is used by doctors in medicine, and to help people who suffer from mental illness. Quite rightly, as we still do not know *how* it works, we must be careful in using it, and this is generally left to those who have studied the subject and who know how to practise it correctly.

Today, when people travel with such speed and comfort from one country or continent to another, the world seems to have shrunk to half its former size. When I was young my parents carried on their business in the Far

East in the great Asian country which is today known as Communist China, and we would travel from seaport to seaport on old-fashioned steamships. There were practically no aeroplanes to carry passengers, very few trains, and only a small number of cars, which could not be of much use because the roads were so bad. In consequence, we went everywhere by ship. It would take us six weeks to travel back to Britain. Yet today, it is possible to fly from China to Britain in less than a day. And because of the speed of travel we have come to think of the earth as a smaller place, but we forget in flying over it so rapidly that below there are still deserts and mountains and jungles which are very lonely places, and that these cover vast areas of land. We forget, too, that the oceans cover more than two-thirds of the earth's surface, and that in places the sea goes down to a depth of several miles. Only in recent times have we been able to dive deeply into it, in submarines and 'submersibles' and other peculiar diving craft. We have only a limited idea of what the deep oceans contain, and there are mountain ranges and forests ashore which are almost impenetrable.

Is it possible that these 'lost worlds' contain new mysteries, to excite and puzzle us? Most scientists, and in particular zoologists, think it unlikely that we will find any very large new types of animal. A great deal of research work has been done in zoology, and most land areas have been visited by scientific people at one time or another, so perhaps they are right. But can we be *sure* they are right?

In the gigantic mountain range to the north of India known to everyone as the Himalaya, which has the tallest mountain in the world, Mount Everest, there have been accounts of huge footprints found in the snow by mountain climbers. Local native people claim to have seen what makes them, too—a great hairy creature, half ape, half man. It has come to be known as 'the Yeti', or more commonly to the outside world as the 'Abominable Snowman'.

I have seen the plaster-cast of one of these footprints, and know a man who was on several of the Yeti expeditions. The footprint measured eighteen inches, and seemed ape-like in outline. The big toe was like that of a chimpanzee, but there are no chimps so high up in the mountains, and their footprint is barely half the size.

No one has photographed a Yeti as far as we know and so much money has been spent in chasing it, without result, that hunters do not bother about it much today. They prefer to let it remain a mystery; but if you question them you will find that most believe it is a real animal which is unknown to science.

While on the subject of giant footprints, it would be as well to mention those found in the great forest-clad mountain areas of the Pacific north-west in the United States, in particular northern California, Oregon and Washington, and in the Canadian province of British Columbia. These states have few roads, and the populations tend to live in the towns and cities as a consequence. Indian tribes have for long known about the 'Giant Man' who makes these footprints, and have given names to him. In Canada he is known as 'the Sasquatch', and in America as 'the Omah', but modern Americans call him 'Big Foot'.

Of course, most people either do not know about these reports or think that they are false, but in recent years so many footprints have been found, measured and photographed, and so many witnesses claim to have seen old 'Big Foot' striding about through the forest lands, it would be unjust to treat them all as liars.

Turning finally to the great water-covered areas of the earth there is one mystery which most people have heard about. It is that of the 'Great Sea Serpent'. Nearly everyone has heard of the half-mythical sea creature which is supposed to swim along exposing a series of curves, or loops of its body, like a row of motor-tyres. It, too, is said to be gigantic—more than 100 feet long on occasion.

Unfortunately, as the seas and oceans are so large the chance of catching one of these sea-serpents is slight, but we can use our brains in finding out whether there really *could* be an unknown type of very large eel, for example, which looked like a sea-serpent. And the answer seems to be 'yes', because not so many years ago baby eels were netted in the ocean which were several feet in length. When you consider that baby eels (or larvae as they are known), offspring of our ordinary 4–5 ft. adult eels, are scarcely an inch or so in length, larvae several feet long could be expected to grow into giants.

And speaking of monsters, there is perhaps the most famous natural-history-mystery of all time to be found within the shores of our own small islands constituting the United Kingdom. I refer of course to the Loch Ness Monster, and as this is of such continuing real interest, the remainder of this book is devoted to its history, the place where people say the Monster lives, and what is being done to try and find out more about it.

# 2

# Scottish Legend of the Water Horse

The strange legend of the Water Horse, or Kelpie, goes far back into history, and may have something to do with the fact that most of the Scottish clans-people lived near to the rivers and lakes which had formed in the valleys.

The whole of northern Scotland has a big rainfall. In consequence there are many rivers and lakes, or lochs as they are known. There are sea-lochs, too, like the fjords of Norway, and 'tarns', or small mountain lakes sometimes referred to as lochans.

The old Highlanders were superstitious people, believing in fairies, witches and demons, who appeared quite real to them, and as they lived close to so much water it was not surprising they invented water-spirits, too, which became a part of the folk-lore as time went by.

Most rivers and springs were known to have their own special guardian spirits, which were kindly creatures, but this was not always true of the deeper lochs and rivers in which might be found other types of mythical creature. Among them was the Water Bull, and Water Horse, or Kelpie.

Researchers have found a pamphlet which describes

them, published as long ago as 1823. In this we are assured the Water Bull was not a fearsome creature. It usually made a home in the smaller lochans, only coming out at night, and not harming anyone.

The Water Horse on the other hand was a dark and evil spirit, in league with the Devil and an enemy of mankind. It was to be found in the lochs and rivers close to routes travellers would take, and it had the unpleasant habit of disguising itself, the better to trick unwary passers-by!

In one such disguise the Kelpie would appear as a fine domesticated horse, complete with silver bridle, and a decorated saddle.

Nibbling the grass peacefully at the roadside it would await the first person to mount its back. The moment this happened the dreadful Kelpie would gallop into the loch, and plunge into the depths, drowning the unfortunate rider. Then, horrors of horrors, it would feed upon the body!

As most people in the Highlands were then of the Catholic faith, they believed that the soul of such a rider must go to Hell if no priest was in attendance at his death to shrive away his mortal sins.

On other occasions it was said that the Water Kelpie used a different disguise. It would come ashore as a handsome young man to beguile the first maiden he could find, and lead her to damnation. But the Kelpie could never hide the wetness of his hair, or the sand and weed entangled in it, and if the maiden noticed this in time there was a chance for her to escape.

In her book *Scottish Folk Tales and Legends*, Barbara Kerr Wilson tells of 'Morag and the Water Horse'. In this story Morag is the beautiful daughter of one Donald McGregor who builds a summer croft-house close to a lonely loch. He did this because he needed to tend his grazing cattle, but his friends advised him against it. They knew for certain that . . . 'a dreaded monster lived in the depths of the great loch, preying on the hillsides round about : a Water Horse! No man could describe the appearance of the monster. Those who had stayed long enough to catch more than a glimpse of the terrible creature, as it rose from the dark waters of the loch, had not lived to tell the tale . . .'

The Water Horse was able to adopt any form at will 'for it was full of evil enchantment' but its normal shape was 'huge and black, and two sharp satanic horns sprang from its monstrous head . . .'

In the story, Morag is visited by a strange but handsome young man when sitting alone one day at her father's summer croft-house. It was bright and sunny, but she noticed at once that his clothes were soaking wet. She asked him why this should be, and he answered telling her that while crossing a burn he had slipped and fallen into the water.

Beguiled by the young man's charm and good looks, Morag offered to comb out his dark tangled locks of hair, to which he at once agreed, laying his head on her lap. But, with each stroke of her comb she found its teeth clogged with weed and silt of the type she had so often seen dragged up from the loch in her father's fishing net . . .

In this particular story there is a happy ending, because Morag recognised her mortal danger just in time. She jumped up, screamed, and took flight, running for her very life, leaping across a burn—a little stream near the cottage—and in so doing shook off her pursuer, because (as is generally known in the Highlands) a Water Horse cannot cross *running* water.

This delightful tale has all the best features a fairy tale should have—mixing beauty and ugliness, goodness and wickedness, trust and terror, in roughly equal proportions, with a happy ending thrown in for good measure. But when it is considered in terms of the Kelpie legend, two facts become obvious.

In the old Highlands of Scotland, something large and frightening, but difficult to describe, lay at the root of these stories. And secondly, it had to do with water—deep water.

The stories that grew up around its appearances were varied, and of course fanciful, but the name given to it is interesting : the 'Water Horse'.

\*       \*       \*

Many books have been published about Scottish folklore, and in *The Highlands and their Legends* by Otta F. Swire, the Water Horse features prominently. It appears in different forms and colours, in different places, and has some peculiar habits. For example, the Water Horse which lives in the River Spey is yellow, and although it used to carry off girls, it now concentrates only on married couples! Another, in Loch Pityoulish, takes the form of a white Highland pony, with a very ornamental saddle and bridle. It specialises in carrying off children who stop to play near the water. It is good at this, and has been known to carry off as many as nine at a time on its back!

In Loch Shin there lives a golden Water Horse, which is known to be the colour of Water Horses in the North and East, whereas black Water Horses are more generally to be found in the West.

In little Loch Borralan the Water Horse is so beautiful fishermen are distracted by it, and as the creature hates to be disturbed it makes off with them. Only their rods and the fish they have caught are left behind, and near them the hoof-prints of a great horse will be found in the mud.

The Great Black Waterhorse of Loch Ness, on the other hand, appears to have received a blessing at one time from St. Columba, who gave it the freedom of Loch Ness for ever for having towed the Saint and his followers from one end of the loch to the other in their coracles— against the wind! It did this by first changing its form to that of an athletic young man, who tied all the coracles' tow-ropes together, then turned back into a Water Horse, and swam off with them trailing behind, the tow-rope in its teeth.

The same Water Horse is also said to have made a pact with the Devil at another time, but was tricked by him, as might be expected.

Altogether, the Water Horse of Loch Ness seems to have been an unusual creature, and of unusual size as Water Horses go, but there have been other good reports about it. For instance, long before the present Benedictine Abbey was built at Fort Augustus at the western end of the loch, St. Cummein founded a religious house for the education and benefit of the local people. He needed to clear the land by plough, but after much hard work his own monks rebelled. It was for them to lead a life of 'teaching and preaching' they said, not digging up rocks. If God needed ploughed land, it was up to Him to provide it!

St. Cummein did not press them, and retired to his cell to pray. The next day a team of red deer came down from the mountain and allowed themselves to be harnessed to the plough. The monks watched in amazement and shame as the stags ploughed steadily throughout the day. Later, when the animals had returned to the mountains with St. Cummein's blessing, and when darkness

23

had fallen, two of the monks arose intent on working at the plough until morning. But the implement had gone from its place at the water's edge, and when they searched for it they found a great black stallion ploughing the field where the deer had been. It was the Water Horse of Loch Ness! By dawn the task was done, and as the sun's rays shone through the mists of morning, the great Beast returned to the loch taking with him a rider on his back: the monk who had tried to 'teach the Lord'.

The first loch to the west of Loch Ness is Loch Oich. Small and shallow, it is connected to its enormous neighbour by the River Oich. It is very beautiful, and the name means quite literally 'The Place of Awe'.

In it there lived another Water Horse, but with a difference—it took no interest in humans whatsoever. Instead, it was known to watch out for deer and sheep, and when these approached the water it would seize them, drag them into the loch, where it then sat on their heads until they drowned!

People claimed to have watched it; what was more, this Water Horse was said to have a peculiar shaped head itself, being flat instead of horse-shaped.

Perhaps at some time previously, it had had its own head sat-upon by some other mythical creature, and was trying to even the score!

No one will ever know for sure.

## 3

# St. Columba and the Loch Ness Monster

When a legend 'comes to life'—and this has happened many times in the past—the usual sequence of events is for the stories and folk-tales to gain support from real evidence. For example, the legendary 'Kraken' was thought to be a myth until the body of a giant squid was finally discovered. This terrible water monster had been described quite accurately by Norwegian fishermen over the centuries, but few believed them. The stories they told of a huge, many-armed monster, with great staring eyes as big as dinner plates, did not impress those who lived safely on land away from the sea. And when reports were made of it actually attacking boats, and even sailing vessels, coiling tentacles about the rigging to pull them over until the gunn'ls were awash, the people ashore just laughed!

Today, we know that the giant squid is real, and that it *has* behaved like this on occasion, though we can only guess at the reason why. Perhaps it is because the giant squid is an enemy of the sperm whale, which feeds on it, and may have attacked the boats out of fear, mistaking them for whales!

The process of legend forming nearly always depends on word-of-mouth to begin with. If an animal-legend has

25

a foundation of fact, as in the case of the 'Kraken', the next step is usually for some educated person to record these stories on paper. Finally, bones, or pieces of skin, hair, or the complete carcass or dead body of the animal is produced for scientists to study. This process often takes a very long time, and as scientists need to be careful before announcing new 'discoveries' (in case they have been fooled by someone playing a practical joke) they are often slow in coming to conclusions. But ultimately, if enough real evidence is produced, a new species of animal is received within the category of scientific zoology.

What this means is that another animal-legend has 'come to life', that it has progressed from the realms of fantasy to become an undisputed scientific fact.

The history of zoology is full of such discoveries, and 'the Kraken' is a good example. It was first reported by fishermen. Next, it was described in writing by an early Norwegian naturalist, Erik Pontoppidan, in his book *The Natural History of Norway*, in 1752. Finally, the body of one was discovered, proving it to be real.

Inevitably, this raises the exciting question in our minds 'can there be any more?' 'Are there any more large unknown animals living on our planet today?'

\*      \*      \*

Bearing in mind the strange tales of the Water Kelpie, and the Great Water Horse of legend in the Scottish Highlands, and the persistent reports of monsters in Loch Ness, we should look next for written evidence; and not just the stories in books and newspapers of today, but accounts from long ago.

We do not have to look far because there is a very clear report in Latin of an encounter with a terrible water monster on Loch Ness fourteen centuries ago. One thousand four hundred years have passed since it was written down. This makes the Loch Ness monster unique, in terms of ancient written history.

To understand this account it is first necessary to examine the life-story of a remarkable man called Columba, or St. Columba as he is known today. He was one of the most daring and successful of the early Christian missionaries to preach in the wild Highlands of Scotland, amongst the pagan tribesmen.

Columba was born in Ireland of Royal blood, in A.D. 521, and in his early life he behaved much as others did in those far-off days, riding, hunting and generally leading an outdoor life. He grew up to be very tall and strong, and to have a powerful voice. He was educated at monastic schools before joining the priesthood himself.

Unfortunately, he became involved in a clan battle in which some 3,000 men were slain, and as it had resulted from his attempts to save a friend who had injured an opponent in a hurling match (a very rough Irish sport) he was blamed, and found it prudent to leave the country. But he was a devout Christian, and a missionary at heart, and when he landed on the tiny island of Iona, off the west coast of northern Scotland, he gained a foothold for the Christian faith by founding a monastery, the remains of which exist today.

Columba was not the first to land on Iona, the Druids having arrived before him, and as they had influence amongst the tribes in Scotland he was fortunate to win the respect and help of one Oran who sent word that Columba should be allowed to speak freely to the tribesmen on his journey eastwards. This opened many doors to him, and the words he preached soon had an effect on the fierce tribesmen who normally distrusted strangers.

In A.D. 565, during one of these missions, Columba travelled up the Great Glen of Scotland towards Inver-

Figure 2 The statue of St. Columba on the east face of St. Benedict's Abbey, Fort Augustus, overlooking Loch Ness

ness, and it was on this journey that we are told he encountered a water monster, at the eastern end of Loch Ness.

An account of this experience was written down in Latin by a man who became the Abbot of Iona after Columba had died, a man called Adamnan who was 'good and wise', and who took the trouble to write a book about St. Columba, who had become very famous during his lifetime.

In Chapter 27 of Book 2 Adamnan has the following to say . . . (as translated simply into English):

'*Of the driving away of a certain Water Monster, by virtue of Prayer, of the Holy Man.* At another time, when the blessed man [meaning Columba] was staying for some days in the province of the Picts, he found it necessary to cross the river Ness—and when he came to the bank he saw some of the local inhabitants burying a poor unfortunate man, who, they said, had been attacked by a water monster, which had bitten him with "a most savage bite". They had set out in a boat to give assistance, but were too late, and the man had died.'

28

'On hearing this Columba directed his companions to swim out and bring over the boat. In response one of them, Lugne Mocumin, stripped off his clothes and dived into the water.

'Now the monster was lying hidden on the bottom, and seeing the water disturbed by the man who was crossing, emerged, and moved towards him with open mouth.

'Then the Blessed man looked on, while all who were there, the heathen as well as the bretheren, were stricken with very great terror; and with his hand raised he formed the sign of the cross, and in the name of God commanded the fierce monster, saying . . . "go no further, nor touch thou that man : *go back at once!*"

'Then the beast on hearing the voice of the saint, was afraid, and fled backwards more rapidly than he came —although it had come so close to Lugne as he swam, there was no more than the length of a punt-pole between the man and the beast.

'Then the bretheren, seeing that the beast had gone away and that their friend was safe, looked in praise and wonder at Columba, and the barbarous heathen who were present, amazed by the miracle they had seen, glorified the God of the Christians.'

By any standard this is a very strange story, but in spite of the centuries that have passed it deserves to be taken seriously, because Adamnan, who wrote the words down in Latin, was a pious and educated man, and he would not have told lies on purpose.

Indeed, he was afraid that people would not believe him at the time, because he introduces the account by saying . . . 'Let no one imagine that I either state a falsehood regarding so great a man, or record anything doubtful or uncertain. Be it known that I will tell with all candour . . . what I have been able to find recorded in the pages written by those who have gone before me, or what I have learned on careful enquiry from certain faithful old men, who told me without hesitation.'

It is likely that this event occurred on or about A.D. 565, some thirty-two years before the death of St. Columba, and if it describes a true experience—then it is a classic of its kind in animal legend-making history.

# 4

## 1933: The Excitement Begins

For uncounted centuries Loch Ness in the Highlands of Scotland was a remote and lonely place, and the surface of this huge body of water was viewed only by the eyes of local fishermen out in their boats, or the occasional traveller making his way from place to place down the line of the Great Glen.

It is the largest of a chain of three lochs which lies in the great trench formed by the rift, or crack in the earth's surface, which divides the Highlands from east to west.

It has more water in it than any other Scottish loch, and at an average 433 feet is very nearly the deepest, too. The walls rise sheer on either side in a series of craggy knolls and precipices which stretch down the length of it, a distance of about twenty-four miles as the crow flies.

A small road was constructed close to the water's edge to form a garrison supply route in the early 18th century. It runs along the south shore east to west about half-way down the loch before slanting away up the mountainside to disappear behind the peaks towards Fort Augustus at the western end of the loch.* This famous little road is

* See map on page 8

31

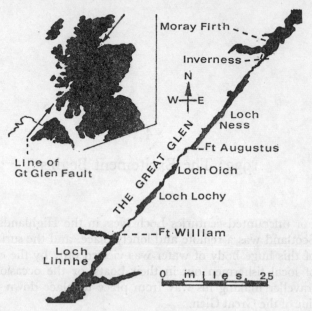

Figure 3 Map of the Great Glen

known as 'General Wade's Military Road' after the army officer who was given the thankless task of constructing it, which he did very well, blasting rocks and obstructions out of the way with black gunpowder. When the job was done, a part of the loch was visible from this road-way, but not many people used it and the trees and bushes soon grew up again, screening off the water.

Along the opposite shore a winding track of a road climbed and plunged up and down the mountainside between the rocks and trees which bordered the loch. Here again, it was possible to travel between Fort Augustus in the west, and Inverness to the east. But it was a long journey and no one made it unless they were mounted on one of the sturdy local ponies, or prepared to take

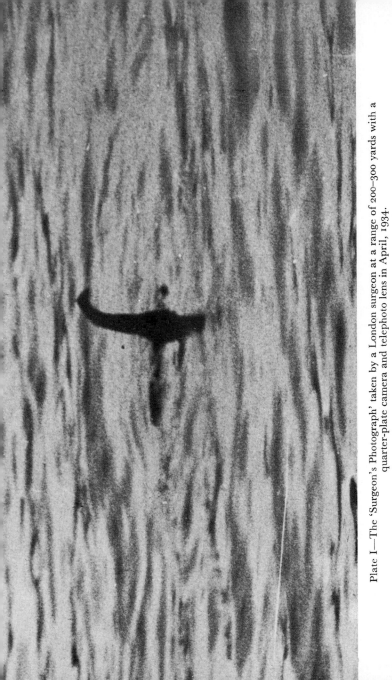

Plate I—The 'Surgeon's Photograph' taken by a London surgeon at a range of 200–300 yards with a quarter-plate camera and telephoto lens in April, 1934.

Plate II—The 'MacNab Picture' taken by Mr. P. A. MacNab with a hand-held camera and 6-inch telephoto lens attached, in the late summer of 1955. Castle Urquhart stands 64 ft high to the right. The object was reported as 'big, undulating and moving at 8–12 knots'; the trigger was released just as the creature was submerging.

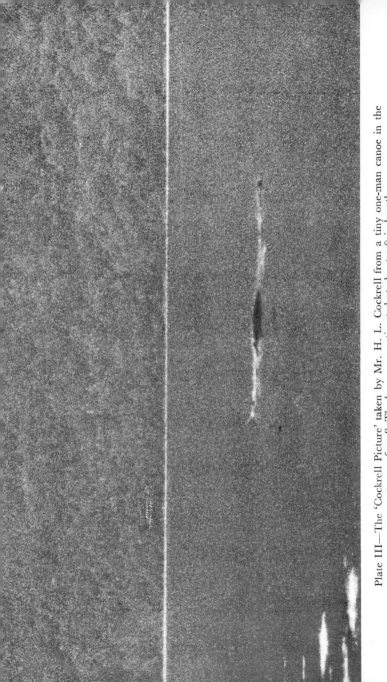

Plate III—The 'Cockrell Picture' taken by Mr. H. L. Cockrell from a tiny one-man canoe in the autumn of 1958. The hump was estimated at about 4 ft in length.

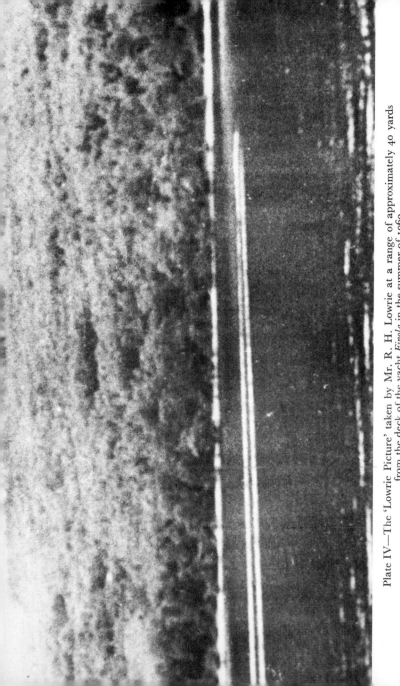

Plate IV—The 'Lowrie Picture' taken by Mr. R. H. Lowrie at a range of approximately 40 yards from the deck of the yacht *Finola* in the summer of 1960.

several days tramping it on foot. Loch Ness, in consequence, was a peaceful place. With the passage of time this road was improved, making it easier for people to pass by the lochside, but it was not until 1933 that any serious attempt was made to build a proper highway—a road which would carry motor-cars and trucks, quickly and directly along the shore in as straight a line as possible. And when this happened, gangs of workmen were brought in, and the trees and bushes that had grown up round the shores in a tangled mass of greenery had to be cleared. More important still, with dynamite available for blasting instead of old-fashioned gunpowder, it was possible to blast a roadway out of the rocky mountainside, making a step, or terrace, for it.

When these operations started the peace and stillness of the ages were shattered. The noise was deafening : explosions shook the ground, hurling rocks and boulders high into the air to fall in spires of foam and cascades of spray into the loch below, the echoes rumbling and reverberating around the mountains, like a summer thunderstorm. The great quantities of rock which had been thrown out plunged down the steep walls of the loch underwater, down into the silt of the bottom hundreds of feet below, creating a disturbance in the black depths of peat-stained water.

In the early summer of 1933 the first reports of something extraordinary began to come in—some strange water-creature of great size was seen occasionally on the surface, or swimming just below it, creating a huge V-wash like a speedboat. No one knew what it was, but as there were so many witnesses the local newspapers began to take an interest.

What could it be, this nameless water-beast with its long thin neck and tiny head attached to a tremendous length of body? No whale, seal or fresh-water fish looked anything like the descriptions made of it. Was it all a lot of nonsense?

Mr. Alex Campbell, the Water Bailie at Fort Augustus, who acted as local correspondent to *The Inverness Courier*, reported on it. If anyone at Loch Ness had the right to comment sensibly it was he, for his whole life was spent on or near the water. As 'Water Bailie' his job was to protect the salmon fishing, and to help in the work of hatching baby fish from the spawn collected from the parents, and thus to build up the stocks of fish in Loch Ness, and other places too, which wanted salmon. His father had been Water Bailie for fifty years before him, and he lived in a cottage only yards away from the lochside.

Alex Campbell had seen this strange creature himself on several occasions in the past, so he did not hesitate to tell the truth about it, and describe what others had reported. The editor of *The Inverness Courier* was impressed, and said 'Well, if the animal is as big as you say it is, then it must be a real *monster*.'

He published an article calling it 'The Loch Ness Monster', and the title stuck. Very quickly the whole world came to know it by this name, and although people have tried to give it a different title since, they have not succeeded. The 'Monster' remains, and is thought of by everyone, everywhere, as belonging to Loch Ness, right up to the present day.

Some people thought it was a bad title, that it was unscientific and embarrassing, but if we look up the word 'Monster' in the dictionary we find that in one sense it is both accurate and descriptive : of the various meanings of the word, two fit very well indeed . . . 'misshapen animal or plant' . . . 'a huge animal or thing'.

Well, the Monster did not appear to be misshapen, though it was peculiar in appearance. It was obviously not a plant, but it most certainly could be described as a 'huge animal or thing', bearing in mind that a 'thing' according to the dictionary is a 'material object'.

Thus no one need have been embarrassed by referring to the Loch Ness Monster as a 'Monster' because that is what it was exactly.

\*       \*       \*

In every great human or scientific drama, there is a point in time when the 'curtain goes up' and the 'first act' commences.

At Loch Ness it occurred with the publication of the 'Mackay' report by *The Inverness Courier* on the 2nd of May, 1933, and it was to be the first of hundreds of similar reports from different people of various nationalities, professions and jobs, from every part of Great Britain, and overseas as well.

The 'first act' of the Loch Ness drama (which is only now approaching its conclusion forty years later) began on a bright, sunlit afternoon at about 3 p.m., with Mr. and Mrs. Mackay driving along the north shore from Inverness.

The water was glass calm, reflecting the clouds above like a huge mirror. At a point almost opposite Aldourie Pier on the opposite shore, Mrs. Mackay caught sight of a violent commotion in the water. At first she thought it must be a couple of wild ducks fighting, but as the disturbance was only about 100 yards away she could see that it was much too big for that. Then the commotion subsided to be replaced by a big wake caused by something large moving just beneath the surface. This began to move quickly away from the shore until at about 450 yards distance two large black humps emerged, moving in line, with the rear one somewhat larger than the first. They rose and sank in an undulating manner, but remained clearly in view. Mrs. Mackay thought the two humps together stretched for about twenty feet. After travelling for some distance towards Aldourie Pier, the humps turned abruptly left, then moved round in a half-circle before sinking, again with a big disturbance.

Mr. Mackay, who was driving, only stopped the car in time to see the final commotion, and the waves the humps had created which came rolling onto the shore.

When this news was published it caused a great deal of interest and curiosity, and before long a flood of similar reports of sightings from people all round the loch came in. The Monster very quickly became the centre of world-wide attention, because although television had not been introduced, radio was common, and everyone listened to 'the News'.

Glancing back through the books and records, it is probable that some twenty or thirty sightings were published in 1933, and that these were only a small part of the total. Due to work on the new road, sightings were often made by groups of people, and they nearly all referred to travelling waves, wakes, and humps of varying numbers, or huge backs; and occasionally a long flexible neck would be seen breaking surface.

Altogether the evidence was impressive, and the scientists of the day did not scoff openly, although many explanations were put forward, none of which seemed to fit the picture. The possibility of a hoax, a sort of large-scale practical joke had to be considered, but who would have the money and the time, and the equipment needed to create such a big disturbance? No one but a millionaire, with a very odd sense of humour!

Perhaps the most important group-sighting in 1933 came from the crewmen of a tug and barge being towed through the loch on October 20th. *Scott II* was a small but powerful vessel owned by the Caledonian Ship Canal authorities, whose canal linked the Ness with the sea to east and west enabling trawlers and yachts and even small ships to sail right through the middle of the Highlands from one coast to another (it saved them the long and dangerous trip round the north-coast, off John o' Groats).

The point about this sighting was that the crew knew what whales and other large sea-animals looked like— the engineer, in particular, a Mr. R. McConnell, was convinced that the object was neither a whale nor a seal. He first noticed a wave-like mound of water moving out from the side of the loch. It seemed to be from something big swimming just beneath the surface, and coming out to look at the two vessels! *Muriel*, the big steel barge, was trailing some distance behind, but on board *Scott II* the engineer called to its mate, Mr. Cameron, who also had a look. Both saw about eight feet of the creature's back, but when McConnell shouted across to the *Muriel*, the Monster sheered away and sank, only to reappear some 200–300 yards astern. All four witnesses, including the skipper and fireman of *Scott II*, saw this reappearance.

The V-wake spreading out from the Monster mingled with the wake from the barge *Muriel*, and Mr. McConnell was sure it could only have been made by something of 'very considerable size'.

Today, some forty years after this event, both the *Scott II* and the *Muriel* can be seen on Loch Ness, or within the Caledonian Ship Canal system. The tug has been refitted with modern diesel engines, and decked out to carry passengers, and old *Muriel* is still used to help in dredging operations. During the summer the now famous tugboat loads up with tourists near Inverness, and makes the trip through the canal to Loch Ness and thence to Urquhart Castle and back. In 1957, she was close to another Monster wake, but this time proof of it was obtained on film through a long-range movie-camera, mounted on the shore.

But to get back to 1933, the *Scott II* sighting was the only one made from boats, but it was certainly not the most peculiar for the year. That distinction went to a company director and his wife, a Mr. and Mrs. G. Spicer, on July 22nd, who reported seeing the Monster in broad daylight, *out of the water*, lurching across the narrow single track of General Wade's Military Road, towards the loch. They were in their car at the time, and nearly ran into it!

On August 4th, *The Inverness Courier* printed a letter from Mr. Spicer, giving details of this experience. It stated that when motoring between Dores and Foyers, something like a 'prehistoric animal' crossed the road about fifty yards ahead. 'It seemed to have a long thin neck, which moved up and down in the manner of a scenic railway, and the body was fairly big with a high back.'

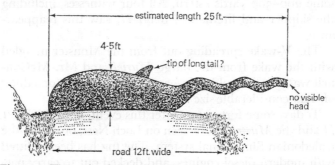

Figure 4 The animal described by Mr. and Mrs. Spicer seen crossing the road near Dores, 22 July 1933

To be truthful, most people (who of course had not met the Spicers) found this account a bit difficult to swallow. There were some who quite definitely thought it was a hoax, and who could blame them? Having the Monster *in* the loch was difficult to believe; to have it prancing about on shore seemed ridiculous.

By now the Loch Ness Monster was causing so much excitement, newspapers began to send their own investigators—people who would try and search out the facts for themselves. The *Daily Mail*, *The Scotsman*, *Le Matin* of Paris, and two Japanese papers from Osaka and Tokyo all sent reporters.

In November, a famous investigator, known to the public as 'Commander Gould', appeared on the scene, commissioned to make his own enquiries and draw his own conclusions. The main reason for this was that Rupert Thomas Gould knew more about reports of giant unknown water animals than anyone living at that time.

His famous book *The Case for the Sea Serpent* published in 1930 earned him a reputation when it first came out.

Commander Gould had spent much of his life in the Royal Navy, and had travelled widely. When he retired in 1927 he took up many hobbies and interests which were unusual, and became an accepted expert in all of them. He was later a member of the BBC's famous radio programme 'The Brains Trust', and his knowledge and experience, not to mention his sense of humour, made him popular with everyone.

He was also a great character, and had the physique to go with it. He stood 6 ft. 4½ inches in his socks, and weighed nearly 250 lb.! To add to all of this he was a keen motorcyclist, and purchased a second-hand bike which carried his enormous bulk twice round Loch Ness during his researches. He christened it *Cynthia*.

After ten days or so of enquiry, Commander Gould wrote a short notice for the Press Association explaining that he had interviewed some fifty witnesses, and come to the conclusion that the so-called 'Loch Ness Monster' was a large living creature of anomalous (meaning abnormal) type, and that it was similar to the unknown sea-animal known generally as the Great Sea Serpent, which was not a serpent at all but an animal with a huge, long body and a snake-like neck which sometimes protruded from the water. He ended by saying 'no other theory can be advanced which covers the whole of the facts'.

Unfortunately, with one or two exceptions, the papers ignored what he had said. In due course, however, he was invited to write an article for *The Times*, and this was published on December 9th, 1933. This produced some 'letters to the editor' which were published for all to read, and many more written privately to Gould himself in which it was made clear that the writers thought he was joking!

In June of 1934 Rupert Gould published his book *The Loch Ness Monster and Others*. Without doubt it was a brilliant piece of work, very much to the point, clear, and original. A model of a book, to which future authors would refer.

The word 'classic' is often mis-used in literature, but in real-life adventure and research, Commander Gould's work had a style about it which was unique. As a result, in 1934, the Monster occupied the thoughts of many learned people, and the first serious attempts to photograph the beast were made.

# 5

# Forty Years of Monster History

In the space of one short chapter it is not possible to record the multitude of events which have taken place over
the forty years since the 1933 sightings; but if we skip
over some of them it should be possible to gain a rough
idea of what has happened.

Better still, if we divide the years into periods of time
we can plot the course the Monster has taken, with all
its ups and downs, and changes in direction.

Summing up the situation one could say that the first
two years of excitement and activity, when the north shore
road was a-building, focussed world attention on the
'phenomenon', as it is sometimes referred to.

From then until the beginning of the Second World
War it was very much in the public eye, but with the
passage of time it began to lose respectability: scientists
began to regard it as a joke, and the Press actively to
treat it as such.

From the end of 1939 when the war started, until vic-
tory was won in 1945, very little was heard of either Loch
Ness or the Monster for the simple reason that the area
had become less easy to visit (fuel for private cars was
rationed and the Royal Navy used the loch for testing
submarines and other equipment).

For the next decade or so, until 1957, when the nation was struggling to get back onto its feet, the loch remained a rather distant place, although the flow of summer visitors slowly began to increase. During this period, the Monster's fortunes were at a very low ebb indeed. Science had long since rejected it, as had the public who now treated it with indifference—a sort of funny story that was no longer original, or amusing. But in spite of this, the Loch Ness Monster refused to die, though officially it was long since 'dead and buried'.

Throughout this whole period of time many apparently truthful accounts had come in, all describing the same thing : huge, unknown water-animals swimming in Loch Ness !

From 1957 to 1962 there was a dramatic change in fortune, and events. It all started with a book written in 1957—*More than a Legend*—which added to the facts about the Monster, or rather *monsters*, because it was obvious there must be several of them living and breeding in the loch.

As a result of this book, some of the men and women who read it became actively interested in the subject, and during the next ten years, until 1972, Loch Ness was the scene of a great voluntary effort to solve the mystery. The story of this research work is still unfolding today.

\*          \*          \*

With this picture-frame of events it is now possible to paint in details, which add colour and depth, and a proper sense of perspective, but to do this we must go back to 1934 because in that year several things happened of importance beyond the run of usual Monster sightings.

Firstly, a hoax, or practical joke, was exposed as such in early January; and as publicity had already been given to it in the Press, this did not help the Monster's reputation.

In December of 1933 a big-game hunter and his assistant searched the shore of the loch and claimed to find tracks of some strange animal which they had never seen before. Fortunately, plaster-casts of these were taken, and proved to be the foot of a hippopotamus, or the print from the dried remains of one. This famous hoax did much to discredit the real evidence which was still coming in.

For example, on January 5th, 1934, a second report of the Monster seen out of water crossing the road was treated with disbelief, and exaggerated by the Press to the point of ridicule. But people who investigated it at first hand came to the conclusion that the eye-witness, a Mr. Grant, was telling the truth about his experience. He really *had* seen a large unknown animal out of water.

To add to the confusion, in April of 1934 a London doctor who was on holiday and touring round the loch stopped close to the water in his car. He saw a disturbance and took several photographs with a plate-camera fitted with a small telephoto lens. When these were developed in Inverness one was found to show what appeared to be the head and neck of the Monster.

The doctor was convinced that the object he had photographed was alive, and no more than 200–300 yards distant. But he had been so busy with the camera that he was unable to describe it in detail.

This picture became known as the 'Surgeon's Photograph', and at the present time is still considered to be a classic, although, as with most of the other evidence, there are people who accept it as genuine, and those who do not. In 1934, however, photography was still in an early stage of development, and by comparison with today's equipment, and standards, it was primitive.

Throughout the year many reports of sightings came in. Alex Campbell, the Water Bailie, collected the names of eighty-two people who claimed to have seen a Monster, and his own was amongst them.

In a letter written to me in 1960 he was kind enough to record the details of his own dramatic experience which occurred early one morning at the western end of Loch Ness. It reads as follows:

'I was standing at the mouth of the River Oich, which flows past my door, one beautiful morning that summer —May if I remember aright, and was gazing across the loch in the direction of Borlum Bay. Suddenly my attention was drawn to a strange object that seemed to shoot out of the calm waters almost opposite the Abbey boathouse. As you can see from the sketch, the swanlike neck reached six feet or so above the water at its highest point, and the body a darkish grey glistening with moisture was *at least* thirty feet long. I gauged this carefully in my mind's eye, by placing two ordinary rowing boats of 15 ft. overall length, end-to-end, and I don't think I was far wrong, because I have had lots of experience of that sort of thing, having lived on the shores of the loch all my life, apart from the last war years.

'Still watching and wondering if I would have time to run for my camera, I heard the noise of the engines of two herring drifters [they call them trawlers in England] which were proceeding down the lower basin of the Caledonian Canal, which enters the loch almost alongside the Abbey boathouse. The animal certainly must have heard, or sensed, the approach of these vessels, too, for I saw it turn its head in an apprehensive way, this way and that, and, apparently being timid, it then sank rapidly out of sight lowering the neck in doing so, and leaving a considerable disturbance on the mirror-like surface of the loch. The animal would have been some 400 yards from where I stood, possibly less, and I had a very clear view of it which lasted several minutes.'

As a result of so many exciting reports about the Monster, rewards were now being offered for its capture. Mr. Bertram Mills, the world-famous circus owner, offered £20,000 for it to be delivered alive to his circus! Another offer of £5,000 was made by the New York Zoological Park, and £1,000 was put up by a private individual. The value of these sums today would perhaps be three or four times as great in terms of the modern pound sterling, which has reduced in value due to inflation. Thus, the prizes were very large and no doubt there were people who would have liked to win them in 1934, which was a time of great industrial depression.

However, not everyone was influenced by money, and one man in particular did something practical about the situation, bearing the cost himself. His name was Sir Edward Mountain.

On 13th July he set up a team of watchers disposed around the loch; armed with binoculars and cameras they kept their eyes on the water between the hours of nine in the morning, and six in the evening.

Altogether, twenty-one photographs were obtained during the first two weeks, of which five were good enough to be enlarged, and later a ten-foot strip of movie-film was added to the collection—not a bad result for a team of only twenty men!

However, the scientists who viewed the results all said they thought the object must be a seal.

How a seal could get into the loch unobserved was not stated, and as was pointed out by an expert on seals who had studied them and lived amongst them in the wild, they do not swim at speed on the surface leaving a large

V-wash. Seals always swim below the surface when moving quickly, and only pop up to breathe.

This unfortunate conclusion had a depressing effect, and no other major expedition was to take to the field for nearly thirty years, partly as a result. People felt that if a team of twenty men working for a month, watching for nine hours a day, could not solve the mystery, there was little hope for individuals, or even a small group of watchers.

The publication of Gould's book *The Loch Ness Monster and Others*, in June of 1934, had influenced a number of serious-minded people, but it did not sell in any great numbers, and was soon out-of-print. It failed to convince many of the sceptics, who did not believe that there could be any unknown animal in a Scottish loch. However, with the passage of years, Gould's work came to be accepted for what it was, a brilliant piece of research, and his reputation did not suffer. In it he referred to his talks with Mr. and Mrs. G. Spicer who claimed to have seen the Monster out-of-water, crossing the road near the village of Dores, and he changed his mind about this truly incredible account. He came to believe them.

He also published details of another 'out-of-water' sighting reported in August of 1933, in which a Mrs. McLennan had described seeing the creature resting on the shore not far from where the Spicers had seen it.

Throughout 1935, much less was heard of the Monster in the news. The new road was through, linking Inverness and Fort Augustus, and the explosions had stopped, to be replaced by the even hum of motor-cars and trucks. The loch had become a peaceful place once more, and there was a reaction in the minds of people everywhere to what was coming to be regarded as a 'silly business'. In spite of the prizes no one had caught a Monster, not even a little one. No one had found any bones or bodily

46

remains . . . and the scientists continued to stay safely away from the place.

Another type of Monster was attracting world-wide attention—a political Monster in the evil form and posturings of Adolf Hitler, and as the storm clouds gathered, the people of Britain began to prepare themselves for what they knew would follow. The Second World War finally broke in thunder and fury in 1939, and for six long years no one had much time to spare for Highland mysteries.

After the war, there was a long period of recovery during which commerce and communications slowly improved. People began to think about their pleasures once again and with the passage of time visitors again travelled up to the Highlands for their holidays, or on business.

But few took the Monster seriously. So much time had gone by it had once again ceased to be a matter of interest. Reports had continued to come in of it, right through from the early 'thirties, but these were generally only mentioned in the local Press. Even a new still photograph obtained by a woodsman in 1951 caused no great excitement. It showed three curious triangular humps, close in to the shoreline, with Urquhart Bay quite clearly in the background.

It would be fair to say that during this twelve-year period, from 1935 to 1947, the Monster had come to be regarded simply as a myth.

However, it was during this time that Mrs. Constance Whyte, M.B., B.S., began her private researches into the subject, ending with the publication of her book *More Than a Legend*, in 1957. Mrs. Whyte was married to the manager of the Caledonian Ship Canal, of which Loch Ness was a part, and lived close to Inverness. Thus she was able to make enquiries herself, and talk to local witnesses.

Her book was read by many people, and as it had been prepared with care and truthfulness, some of these people became so interested in the subject that they began to investigate it for themselves.

A Highlander named Torquil MacLeod, and his Australian wife 'Liz', who enjoyed a sense of adventure, were the first to become full-time Monster-hunters. They sold the two-masted ketch *Airy Mouse* on which they had been living, and bought a large war-surplus radio truck. They drove it up to Loch Ness, and round the shores for six months, making a home in it, before renting a croft-house high up in the mountains.

Unhappily Torquil only lived two years, as he was suffering from a rare form of blood disease; but during that time he and Liz were busy, and on one occasion in 1960 they were both witness to a monster-surfacing, which was watched, and photographed, from a large yacht in transit through the loch. It became known as the 'Lowrie' sighting, after the name of the family on the yacht, who were too close to the Monster for comfort ! It was so huge, and 'sinister', that they decided to heave-to so as not to collide with it. At forty yards distance they could not be mistaken about it either, as their photograph was to prove. It showed a large V-wash on glassy-calm water, but the three humps, and the huge body underwater which they could see from the deck did not show up well in the picture.

Earlier in the year Torquil had seen the Monster out-of-water, across the loch, and had studied it for nine minutes through binoculars, and although he was alone at the time, he was able to give a good account of it and to measure it quite accurately through the 'graticulations' or marks on the lens of his binoculars. He decided the creature was between forty-five and fifty-five feet long, not counting the back-end which was still in the water. It

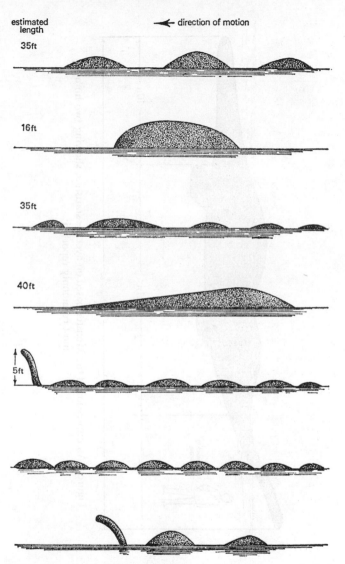

estimated
length

35ft

16ft

35ft

40ft

5ft

← direction of motion

Figure 5 Various body shapes sketched or photographed by
different observers

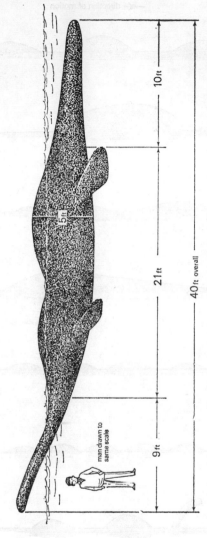

man drawn to same scale

9ft

21ft

40ft overall

5ft

10ft

Figure 6 An impression of the Monster based on average statistics, showing two humps most commonly reported

was lying on the rocky edge of the loch, and was quite evidently alive, because it finally turned half round and re-entered the water. It had a long neck like an 'elephant's trunk', and a huge body and two pairs of limbs. The rearmost quite clearly like great paddles.

In 1959 I had become interested in the Monster myself, and had spent many months studying the subject and analysing details. It seemed to me there could only be three possibilities : people were either telling fibs; or, they were simply mistaken in what they had seen; or, they were telling the truth quite accurately.

I felt compelled to try and find out which answer was the correct one.

Over a period of about five months I was able to collect one hundred separate eye-witness reports from different sources, and study these in detail. I drew up a large paper chart with headings, and under each wrote in what people had said about their experience. Each heading covered just a part of the whole experience. For instance, if people were clear about a part of the Monster they had seen—its head, or flippers, or the way it swam or dived—these bits of information went in under the correct heading.

Altogether, there were twenty-two headings, and by the time the study was complete there were many yards of paper attached. The whole job proved very interesting, and as I progressed with it, it became clear that the Monster really was a living animal. I could scarcely believe it, because it was like proving that a Unicorn existed! And yet, I could not doubt the truth of what I had read and analysed so carefully.

Obviously the next step was to travel up to Loch Ness, and to see if I could obtain some fresh evidence on film. I could not get away until April of 1960, but in that month I loaded up my small car with cameras and tripods, a folding canoe, equipment and supplies, and set forth on the 600-mile journey. In those days the roads had not been improved much, and it took a long time to get there.

When I did, late on the second evening, Loch Ness greeted me with uncanny stillness and beauty; and stretching far into the distance the dark mountains and the great shining pool of water were lit by the fading rays of a wintry sun. It was unreal. It appeared to beckon me, and yet to hold a warning which sent chills up and down my spine . . . It was mysterious, and lonely and magnificent!

Driving on, I spent the night at a small hotel on the south shore, about halfway down the loch, then started to hunt in earnest, rising at dawn each morning, and travelling round the loch to places of advantage from which I could scan the water.

It was a huge lake, nearly seventy miles round by road, as I soon discovered in my search for local witnesses—people like Alex Campbell, the Water Bailie, who could tell me of their experience at first-hand.

Talking to these quiet Highlanders was encouraging because it was obvious they were telling the truth. It was most exciting, too, because what they described was the Monster I had learned about on paper; but their experiences brought it to life for me.

I decided to redouble my efforts with the long-range movie-camera, which I set up each morning at different places around the loch, watching through the hours of daylight, scanning the waters with binoculars.

After three days of this, without result, a man staying at the Foyers hotel on holiday told me that he had seen a huge V-wake travelling down the loch about half-a-mile distant. There was nothing visible making it, and as no ordinary fish in the loch could make a disturbance like that, I realised that at least one Monster was still alive and kicking! This was an exciting moment. Then on the evening following I saw a disturbance (but not a V-wake) off the mouth of the River Foyers. I shot some film of it in bad light, and later, when the film was developed, it proved to be a patch of rough water caused by waves breaking over a shoal of rocks, just under the surface.

I was not to know that at the time, however, and continued with my expedition for another three days.

Early on the Saturday morning of April 23rd, 1960, returning from a dawn-watch further down the loch, I spotted something large far out on the water.

I was in my car, with the camera mounted on a tripod beside me in place of the front seat which I had removed. I was overlooking Foyers Bay at a point about 300 ft. up the mountainside. It was just before nine o'clock, and the water was calm, and the air clear as crystal.

The sun shone on the object, and I could see it was a reddish-brown colour.

Stopping the car at the roadside I lifted my binoculars and examined it carefully. Enlarged seven times, I could see it much better. It was not a boat, and it was quite motionless.

Suddenly it came to life, and surged away across the water, with ripples breaking away from the farther end. I could see now that it was the back of a great animal—a strange humped back, and on the left side of it there was a curious dark blotch. There was no fin on the back— as with a whale, or a porpoise—of that I was certain.

Turning to my camera, I shot about forty feet of film of the Monster as it zig-zagged its way across the loch, gradually submerging.

When fully submerged it turned abruptly left underwater, and swam close to the far shore for perhaps a quarter of a mile, throwing up the great V-wash I had read about, and which the man had described to me three days previously.

With only fifteen feet of film remaining, I stopped the camera, and raced with it in the car down the mountain-side, out over a field towards the shore hoping to get a much closer view of the Monster; but when I arrived at the water's edge there was nothing to be seen for miles in each direction—just the glassy surface. The Monster had dived back into the depths!

Disappointed, I returned to eat my breakfast, then arranged for the hotel owner to take out a rowing-boat with a small outboard engine, so that I could film it for comparison. Obviously, if a boat of the kind used on Loch Ness appeared in the same film, after the Monster, it would at least prove the object wasn't a boat. This comparison was vitally important.

Later, back in England, I had the film developed carefully by Kodak, and in the weeks that followed it was shown privately to a number of people; but it was not until it was seen on television—on Richard Dimbleby's famous *Panorama* programme of June 13th, 1960—that the Loch Ness Monster again became a matter of popular interest and serious discussion.

Nearly ten million people had watched the interview, and seen the film for themselves.

\*     \*     \*

In the years that followed, right up to the present day, voluntary watchers and researchers began to visit Loch Ness in ever-increasing numbers. The story of this is exciting, but it is best dealt with in Part II of this book—'Hunting the Monster'.

# 6

## Some Monster Questionmarks

The question of what the Monster really looks like is probably the first that springs to mind, assuming that people believe that there is a Monster in Loch Ness. There are a great many who do not, and this is understandable, because they are not aware of the facts concerning it, and in consequence treat the matter lightly.

What it looks like is important, certainly, but before discussing this perhaps it would make better sense to examine other aspects of the case, and to ask some other equally important questions first.

For example, there is no point in discussing a Monster of any kind, if it was impossible for one to have got into the loch in the first place. Thus, we should start by asking the question 'Where could it have come from?'

The answer is simple: if it is real, and a large water animal, then it must have come from the sea.

The next question as to how it could have done this is not so easy to answer, because Loch Ness is now fifty feet above sea-level, and nearly seven miles away from the sea. However, as far as we know it was an arm of the sea *since* the time of the last Ice Age; just like a Norwegian fjord, it was a salt-water inlet, and sea animals would have swum in and out of it.

Then, as far as we know, the land began to rise very, very slowly, just as it is doing today, at the rate of one millimetre per year. This does not sound much, but when thinking in terms of thousands of years, the rise becomes considerable.

Thus, one might have expected a sand-bar to begin to form at the end of Loch Ness fjord, over which these sea animals would swim at first without much difficulty; but as more centuries passed it would cause an obstruction, and as time went by they must have found it troublesome to cross, and ultimately they would not be able to.

Next, they would find that the deep trench of the Ness contained enough water for them, and enough fishlife to feed upon. More centuries would pass, and the fjord, or sea-loch, would turn into an ordinary loch, cut off from the sea by a solid piece of land, across which a short river would make its way, draining the surplus water from the loch.

As more time went by the salt water in the loch would become diluted by the fresh rainwater running into it, and these sea animals would slowly get used to it, or in terms of evolution, they would begin to *adapt* to the new environment. After thousands of years the loch might be several miles from the sea, and now quite fresh, and the sea animals in it managing to live quite comfortably.

It is a remarkable fact that adaptations of this kind in nature have occurred in many different places, and with many different species of animal. It is quite possible for it to happen, if enough time is allowed to go by.

In Lake Tung-Ting in China, 650 miles from the mouth of that huge river the Yangtze Kiang, there is a species of dolphin living and breeding in fresh water. In Lake Nicaragua, in Central America, there is a species of fresh-water shark which is dangerous to man. It must also have been cut off from the sea, and has learned to adapt. Nature is both marvellous and adaptable in the most astonishing ways. Only recently a species of beetle has been found living in Alaska, which freezes solid during the long arctic winter, only to come back to life when the temperature rises in the summer! Technically, it should die when it is frozen, but it does not, and the scientists have found a substance in its body fluids which resists freezing, like the anti-freeze we put into a car radiator! Animals adapt to their environment, through the evolutionary process.

But if the Loch Ness Monsters have adapted to their fresh-water environment, and they obviously have, is there any chance that they could get out of the loch by underground channels, or an underground river, bearing in mind that the whole area of the Great Glen, of which Loch Ness forms part, is a colossal fault zone, or crack in the earth's surface? The answer to this must be 'yes, it is possible, but extremely unlikely'. For today, Loch Ness is a long way from the sea—there would need to be a seven mile tunnel, or underground river connecting the two, and as the loch is now fifty feet above sea-level, unless this passageway had ups and downs in it which only allowed water to flow out in flood conditions, there would be a constant rush of water through it, draining from the higher level and head of pressure in Loch Ness.

With all enquiries, one good question leads to another, and as this is a stimulating process and the best way of finding out what we know about Monsters, it would save space to proceed on a simple question-and-answer basis, bearing in mind that we are still very ignorant about many things. We can, however, make suggestions, and intelligent guesses where we do not have the answers . . .
Q. If the Loch Ness Monsters came from the sea originally, what sort of animals are they?

A. At the present time we do not know, and can only theorise, but of the five theories put forward each has some good points in favour of it, and some bad ones against it, technically. None of them seems to fit the reported evidence in every detail. Perhaps a better way to arrive at an answer is to eliminate those known water-animals which do not appear to fit the evidence at all. According to Commander Gould, who had wide experience, these include salmon, otter, porpoise, tortoise, turtle, aquatic birds, eel, ribbonfish, any known species of whale, or seal (including walrus, sea-lion, sea-leopard and sea-elephant), sturgeon, crocodile, shark, sunfish, ray, and giant squid.

With these interesting creatures out of the way, we are left with the five theories which suggest the presence of a currently *unknown* species of mammal, reptile, fish, amphibian or invertebrate!

For example, if it is a mammal could it be a species of giant, long-necked seal? Or if a reptile, a survival from the past, a species of long-necked plesiosaur, the forebears of which swam in the oceans 70,000,000 years ago?

The only way to find out which of these theories is nearest to the truth is to study the Monster's history, and in particular the new results from expeditions.

Q. What would the Monsters eat? What food supply is available to them in Loch Ness?

A. There is very little weed in or around the loch, so that it is unlikely the creatures are herbivores.

The waters contain abundant plankton, however, and these microscopic creatures feed the fish, of which there are great numbers in the loch.

Salmon are frequently caught weighing thirty pounds or more, migrating up from the sea. Trout are numerous, too, and grow to abnormal size of up to twenty pounds. Pike of varying size inhabit the river mouths, and vast

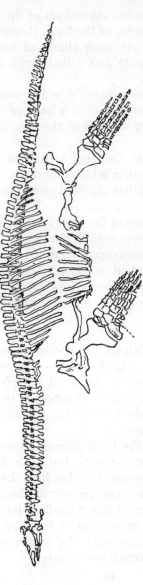

Figure 7 Skeleton of a typical long-necked plesiosaur, thought to have become extinct 70,000,000 years ago

numbers of eels live in the bottom silt of the shallow bay areas, and along the sides of the loch. Recently evidence has also been found on sonar charts of some very big shoals of deep-swimming fish called arctic char, which weigh a pound or two.

Quite obviously fish provide a ready source of food supply, and as the Monsters have a habit of 'dashing off' as though in pursuit of something, they could be chasing fish.

They do not possess the large head and mouth of a typical plankton-eater (like a Greenland whale or a basking shark), and no one has reported one of them munching weed.

Q. Having covered some of the basic questions, we should now ask what the Monster really looks like.

A. The best way to construct a picture is to study what the eye-witnesses have had to say, and also the films and photographs. Judging eye-witness reports is a slow and laborious task, but it outlines a picture which is surprisingly detailed.

*The Head:* Starting with the head, various accounts have been made by people who have seen it at close range; and as might be expected, heads of differing sizes are described. If there are young Monsters in the loch, and adult males, and females too, we can expect to see some differences amongst them.

With many reports the head appears so small that it's almost an extension of the neck, but with the very big Monsters a typical account describes it as the 'head of a calf, only flatter'. If one can picture the head of a calf, with its cranium flattened like a shallow inverted bowl, this may give a good impression of it. Some people say that the head is 'definitely snake-like' and most who have had a good view agree that it is very ugly.

Sometimes, on top of the head two small projections are seen like the 'horns on a snail', and the eyes (which are not often seen) are like 'slits in a darning needle', and they are 'bright and glittering'.

*Neck:* The neck is long and flexible, and very muscular, varing from two or three feet to as much as ten feet in length, and a foot in diameter. On occasions too, people have described a curious mane-like appendage hanging down the back of the neck like sea-weed, only it does not appear to be weed of any kind, but a part of the animal.

*Body and Tail:* The body is long and flexible. In the reports of big animals it must be colossal, perhaps forty or fifty feet in length, protruding several feet out of water at the humps; and at the rear there appears to be a broad rudder-like tail, which is used in propelling the creature through the water, like the tail of a crocodile . . . 'I saw the tail distinctly causing a great commotion, thrashing the water with much force', is one such description.

*Humps:* One of the oddest features of all is the humps on the back of the Monster, referred to in so many reports. These vary in size, shape and number, and sometimes no humps are seen but just a huge back like an 'upturned boat'. Sometimes triangular humps are seen, and sometimes rounded humps, or long flattened humps. Most peculiar of all, people have actually reported the humps *changing shape*. It is all very puzzling, but as they exist there must be an explanation for them. Could it be that there are two or three basic humps and an inflatable organ along the back which alters shape as it inflates with air, or possibly even water? Some animals have developed external air sacs or skin pouches which are useful to them. At the present stage of investigation we can only guess at the true nature of the Monster's extraordinary humps which appear in the films and the still photographs which have been taken of it.

*Limbs:* On either side of the Monster people have seen limbs, or paddles, or flippers. The rear ones seem to be bigger than the fore-limbs, which have been described both as 'stumpy legs', and 'squarish-ended flippers'. Many land animals which have taken to the water have evolved webbed toes, and ultimately their feet have become adapted into paddles. This process, of course, takes millions of years and in some cases the limbs can serve a double purpose, helping the creature overland, and in swimming, too.

*Skin:* The skin of the Monster has been described in different terms by witnesses, but those who have had a close sighting have generally agreed that it is rough, or warted like the skin of a great toad. At a distance, when the sun is shining on a wet surface it may appear shiny and smooth, but at close quarters this optical illusion cannot happen. No one has described the skin as being scaly, and although there have been many reports which simply describe the Monster as looking 'dark' or 'black', of those which report a definite colour, about half say it is elephant, or battleship grey, and half that it is a reddish-brown. Sometimes, too, blotches are seen—areas of darker shading, like the dapple on a cow.

This roughly is what witnesses have to say about the Monster, and although it has been reported out of water by a number of different people, with one or two exceptions these encounters have been brief, and only a glimpse of it has been obtained. On two occasions, however, the witnesses have had time to study the Monster on shore at a distance through binoculars. Once, for a period of twenty-five minutes during which time the creature remained continuously clear of the water, and once for eight or nine minutes. In both cases the Monster lay on the shore, only partly out of the water, and displayed a long neck.

In the latter case, I knew the witness personally. He was a friend whom I both admired, and trusted, and who spent the last two years of his life on research at Loch Ness—the 'Torquil MacLeod' to whom reference is made in Chapter 5. He very kindly sent me his account and sketches on the 19th September, 1960, and I was able to publish these in 1961.

A shortened version reads as follows :

'At approximately 3.30–3.45 p.m. on February 28th, 1960, I was driving towards Fort Augustus, when approximately $2\frac{1}{2}$ miles from Invermoriston, I had occasion to pull up, and my attention was attracted by a slight movement upon the opposite shore [there is no road along this stretch]. The weather was dull and overcast, with a drizzle drifting down the loch . . .

'Upon turning my glasses on the moving object, I saw a large grey-black mass (I am inclined to think the skin was wet and dry in patches) and at the front there was what looked like an outsize in elephant trunks. Paddles were visible on both sides, but only at what I presumed was the rear end, and it was this end (remote from the "trunk") which tapered off into the water.

'For about 8 or 9 minutes the animal remained quite still, but for its "trunk" (I assume neck, although I could not recognise a head as such), which occasionally moved from side to side with a slight up-and-down motion—just like a snake about to strike, but quite slowly. It was

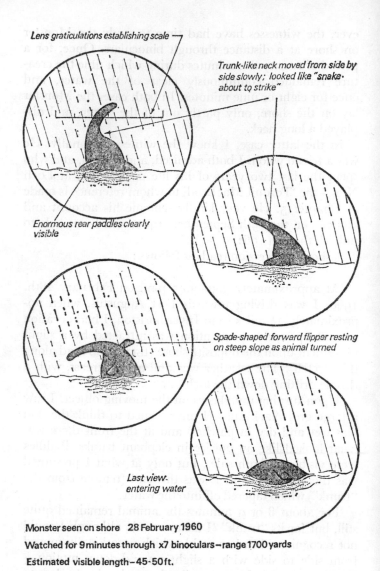

Lens graticulations establishing scale

Trunk-like neck moved from side by side slowly; looked like "snake about to strike"

Enormous rear paddles clearly visible

Spade-shaped forward flipper resting on steep slope as animal turned

Last view entering water

Monster seen on shore 28 February 1960

Watched for 9 minutes through x7 binoculars – range 1700 yards

Estimated visible length – 45-50 ft.

Figure 8 Sketches drawn by Torquil MacLeod of his sighting, 28 February 1960

to my mind obviously scanning the shores of the loch in each direction.

'In the end it made a sort of half jump, half lurch to the left, its "trunk" coming right round until it was facing me, when it flopped into the water and apparently went straight down; so it must be very deep close inshore at this point. As it turned I distinctly saw a large squarish-ended flipper *forward* of the big rear paddles, or flippers: call them what you will but *not* legs. I did not see the end of the tail at any time, but the animal looked something like this . . .' [See Figure 8]

Torquil Macleod's 'glasses' were Ross 7 x 50 binoculars of good quality, with graticulations. As already stated he was able to use these to measure the Monster's length, and came up with a figure of forty-five to fifty-five feet for those parts of the creature which were actually out of water.

He ended his letter to me with these remarks . . . 'That's about all I can tell you, and conditions were by no means ideal. I think the L.N.M. looks like this . . .'

Figure 9 Torquil MacLeod's impression of the Monster

Q. One last question—if the Monster can remain clear of the water for up to ten minutes or more, surely it must breathe air? Is there any evidence for this?

A. This is an important question. How does the Monster breathe? Is it through gills, or through its skin, or through some other bodily organ? We simply do not know. If it has lungs, then it must inhale and exhale air periodically, and with such a *huge* animal one would think the sound of this would be heard. But in fourteen years of research at Loch Ness I have only come across four reports of sounds which could be of the Monster breathing, and only one report of the head seen on the surface with the mouth opening and closing regularly, 'as though it was breathing'. However, bearing in mind the size of the loch, and the rare appearances of the Monster, and the even rarer close-up sightings, these few reports are understandable. Perhaps the most significant thing about them is that they seem to describe definite breathing noises. Like a 'great horse snorting' is one description; and a 'puffing noise like a school of porpoises' is another.

In November of 1972 I visited Tyne-Tees Television for an interview with Mr. Hughie Green about the Monster. As a result of it a number of viewers wrote in, and amongst these letters were two which recorded new 'wake' sightings from Loch Ness, and one of an astonishing encounter with a huge unknown sea-creature off Limerick, on the west coast of Ireland. This letter was from a Mr. E. A. Aldridge, living in Gloucestershire, and dated 30th November, 1972 . . .

'Watching your programme "Sky's the Limit" as I usually do, I was very interested about the Loch Ness Monster; and I now quote from the memoirs of my uncle, Captain Hugh Shaw, who was a coastwise schooner-owner and master for some years off the coast of the U.K. This concerns a trip to Limerick on the west coast of Ireland around 1922. I quote: *We had finished*

66

*loading and we were ready to sail, and it was near high-*
*water in the afternoon. I was down in the cabin, writing.*
*My mate suddenly called to me in a very excited voice . . .*
*"Captain! Come up here at once!"*

'When I reached the deck, I saw the quays on both sides
of the river crowded with people, and then I saw the
reason for this. They were watching the most amazing
sea-creature they or I had ever seen or read about. This
object was close alongside my vessel, in fact it was only
a few feet away. My first impression on seeing it was of
its resemblance in size and shape to a small submarine.
It was large and black and shining, and it had a very
long neck at least twelve feet long, held proudly erect
and shaped like a swan's. It waved its smallish head from
side to side, and its bright shining eyes seemed to express
alarm.

'Behind its long neck for a distance of about ten or
twelve feet was a massive black cone-shaped hump, which
rose a few feet out of the water, but no part of the creature's body could be seen between the hump and the neck,
this part being submerged. It was heading upstream at
a very slow speed. All the seabirds resting on the buoys
flew away as the creature came near to them. Several
people watching near my vessel called to me, to ask could
I tell them what it was, but of course I could not enlighten
them.

'After it passed my ship, it saw the bridge, close to and
straight ahead of it, and with movements like a stately
ship, it made a left-handed turn. It did not hurry. It
now began to head downstream, and as it passed some
yachts anchored across from where we lay, I was better
able by comparison to estimate the height of its neck and
hump, also its entire length. Passing one yacht, when its
head was in line with the yacht's mast, the head was half-
way up the topmast, and when the neck was showing

67

*clear of the yacht's stern, the mid hump was halfway up the yacht's lower mast. It continued on its way downstream, gathering speed as it cleared the narrows.*

'*One hour later we left on our way to sea. After we had passed Hoynes, which is about twenty miles below Limerick, it was nearly dark when I and my crew heard a blowing sound, like a porpoise makes when it surfaces for air, and we saw the long neck of the sea creature shoot out of the water; then it disappeared. It returned within a few seconds, surfacing to blow and take in air again. This it did again and again. It then dropped astern as it was not travelling as fast as our vessel was motoring.*

'*That was the last we saw of it.*'

It is important to note that the River Shannon, which is tidal at the mouth, is open to the sea through the estuary thirty to forty miles in length, which would be referred to as a sea-loch in Scotland, and a fjord in Norway, and that reports of similar animals have come from both these other types of inlet, too. Also, in the film I shot in 1960 there is a large conical-shaped hump which is seen to move through the waters of Loch Ness, as it gradually submerges.

But in order to up-date the Loch Ness reports we can do no better than quote from the two other letters sent to Mr. Hughie Green, who kindly forwarded them to me. The first was written on 4th December, 1972, from a Mrs. Kay Shakespeare, of Nottingham . . .

'. . . During our holidays in August, 1955, my husband and I had the experience of seeing what we could only take to be an extremely long, powerful creature swimming down the centre of the loch (we were near Foyers), and the wash it created could *not* have been caused by

68

anything else, as it was one of those hot airless days that one sometimes gets in the Highlands, and there wasn't a boat or anything else in sight. Of course, although up to that time on our frequent visits to Scotland we had been extremely sceptical about the whole thing, we were, and still are, absolutely convinced that there is a very large creature (or indeed, creatures), and are only waiting for the real proof to be found.

'When we told the local Press at Inverness about it, they were more concerned as to whether my husband was pulling their leg about his name William Harold Shakespeare. In fact when he returned to work, one of his mates had written on the floor in large print, "A MID-SUMMERNIGHT'S DREAM".'

The second letter was from a Mrs. E. Essex, written on December 2nd, 1972 ...

'I have no question to ask, but we, too, had an uncanny experience at Loch Ness this year. A party of us had just parked our cars on the opposite side of the castle; getting out, we immediately said "Well, where is he?", meaning the Monster.

'Someone pointed out to the loch, and there sure enough was something travelling through the water; it was definitely not a boat giving off a wake. We watched it spell-bound; no one spoke, and it moved from in front of us, until out of sight to the left.

'A few minutes later an eerie silence; then waves lapped against the shore with great force. Someone said it was "shaking a leg" and we all laughed . . . I swear if there is a monster there, we saw it in early August. It was an unforgettable experience.'

During the course of the TV programme, Hughie

Green had mentioned that while passing through Loch Ness in his own boat he spent a night moored at Urquhart Bay; and that early in the morning the craft had been rocked by ripples which had come out of nowhere. This is an experience I have also had when living on the water in boats on Loch Ness. It is most peculiar, and the ripples are big enough to rule out any fresh-water fish.

The last time it happened was in Dores Bay, early one mist-enshrouded, breathless morning in October, 1972. Unfortunately, I was alone aboard so there was no witness, but I had no doubt that the disturbance had been caused by something large moving through the water. It was too early for boats to be passing through the loch, and the dense mist would have put a stop to navigation.

# 7

# The Evidence on Record

When studying the facts of any controversial subject it is helpful to know what has already been published and what films and photographs exist. In the case of the Loch Ness Monster there is plenty of evidence in writing; a number of still photographs, and a few films—all of which deserve to be considered. In recent years, too, many hours of tape-recordings have been made of new sighting reports, and of old ones, from witnesses who have only recently come forward. These tapes are intriguing, as they carry the inflexions of voice, dialect, and tone which bring them to life. But, of all the evidence, the photographs and films are the most exciting, as they help to construct a picture of the beast.

Unfortunately, there may well be photographs which have never been published. Not everyone realises the significance of what they have seen, and in some cases photographed . . . and we can only hope that as time passes there will be less ridicule surrounding the Monster, and that witnesses will not be afraid to admit to their experience. There are signs that this is happening today, and it is a great encouragement to the researchers.

*Books of Reference*
As already noted, Lieut.-Commander R. T. Gould was the first author to write a book on this subject, based on his own observations and research around the loch. *The Loch Ness Monster and Others* was published by Geoffrey Bles in June, 1934, setting the pace for future Monster-hunters. As a first edition, it soon went out-of-print in Britain, but today it has been reprinted in the United States, with other of his works which are now regarded as classics.

Next to appear was *More than a Legend* in 1957, by Constance Whyte, M.B., B.S. Hamish Hamilton, the publishers, reprinted this in 1958. This book was considered to be a brilliant contribution, coming at a time when the Monster was very much in need of support.

In 1961, Routledge and Kegan Paul, Ltd., ventured into print with *Loch Ness Monster*, by myself. It was the first book to be written by someone who had actually *seen* the beast, and it survived to appear in America the following year, published by Chilton Books, Inc. Routledge reprinted in 1966, then published a new edition in paperback in 1972, bringing the story up-to-date.

Later in 1961, Rupert Hart Davis, Ltd., published *The Elusive Monster*, by Maurice Burton, D.S.C., in which various alternative theories were put forward in explanation of the Monster's appearance, including vegetable-mats, and long-necked otters.

In 1966, Routledge & Kegan Paul published my second book in the series, *The Leviathans*. This was brought up-to-date in 1972 as a new edition by Acropolis Books, Ltd., in the United States, under the title *Monster Hunt*.

In 1968, Faber & Faber, Ltd. published *The Great Orm of Loch Ness*, by F. W. Holiday, the well-known fishing writer. This subsequently went into paperback in 1971, and found a wide market. It was the first book to put forward the 'invertebrate' theory, and covers folk-lore internationally in respect of 'Orms' (the name given to the Loch Ness and kindred monsters by its author).

In July, 1972, for the first time a book was published about the research work done by the Loch Morar Survey team of young scientists. Elizabeth Montgomery Campbell contributed ten of the fourteen chapters, and Dr. David Solomon—three chapters. Both writers co-operated to complete the final chapter of *The Search for Morag*. Tom Stacey, Ltd., published this important book in Britain, and Walker and Company plan to do so in the United States, in 1973. 'Morag' is the nickname given to the Loch Morar Monster, just as 'Nessie' is the popular title for its cousin in Loch Ness.

### Books for Young People
This book is the first to have been written seriously about the Monster for young people, and no doubt there will be others to follow by different authors. One of the most encouraging aspects of research into the unknown is that as progress is made more and more information becomes available for publication. Ultimately, the facts, whatever they are, become accepted. If they are real, and can be proved, the subject then becomes respectable!

### Press coverage
Since 1933 the Press in Britain and abroad has published countless news items on the Monster, and a great number of magazine articles has appeared over the years. Some have been factual and sensible, and of a high journalistic standard; and others have printed unmitigated rubbish.

We must accept that newspaper editors are looking for news, and in particular dramatic stories, but they often introduce the subject of the Monster with a funny headline, or a cartoon. In view of the hoaxes that have occurred at Loch Ness, this is to some extent excusable, but ill informed; sloppy reporting is not. One can only hope that as the subject comes to be recognised for what it truly is, a most important and exciting natural discovery, it will be treated more seriously.

In reporting evidence accurately the Press does not have an unblemished record, but it never fails to act quickly, and to be inquisitive, which is one of its most important functions in any free society.

In the published record, too, we must reserve a place for the writers who contribute ideas, and summarise information in booklets at a price the public can afford. Amongst them, Fr. J. A. Carruth, M.A., at St. Benedict's Abbey, Fort Augustus, whose annually up-dated booklet *Loch Ness and its Monster* is sold at the Abbey shop for the benefit of charity.

## Tape-recordings

Since the invention of small, portable cassette tape-recorders a few years ago, verbal evidence-getting has been made easier. One can now record a witness without fuss or embarrassment by simply pressing a switch!

Obviously tapes of this kind can be used for radio programmes, and several have already been published in this way. But their real value is in making records which can be stored indefinitely and played back at any time to capture the sounds, comments and excitements of the moment. No good Monster-hunter should be without a cassette tape-recorder.

## Films and Photographs

The first still photograph published of the Loch Ness Monster (that we know about) was taken by a Mr. Hugh Gray one Sunday in November, 1933. It was one of five pictures taken, four of which apparently did not come out at all. I met and talked to Mr. Gray at Foyers on the south shore of Loch Ness, in April, 1960, on my first expedition, and he took me out to where he claimed to have seen first a huge disturbance, then about forty feet of back, and a powerful tail which lashed about causing so much spray it was difficult to distinguish details.

The picture appeared in Commander Gould's book, in 1934, and in the copy I have it does not show very much of anything. The print has either been touched up to create the impression of spray, or light has spoiled the picture. There are other features in it which are peculiar, and although in 1968 F. W. Holiday described it as 'the most detailed photograph so far obtained' I have yet to find a photographer who could agree with him; indeed, on page 23 of his own book Gould refers to the 'vague outlines of the original'!

*The 'Irvine Films': 1933 and 1936*
A second picture—a still from a short film exposed off Inverfarigaig, on December 12th, 1933—also appeared in Gould's book. It showed a long, dark shadow on a water surface; but it cannot be judged without projecting the film from which it was printed. Constance Whyte refers to a second film of the Monster taken in 1936 by the same photographer, a Mr. Malcolm Irvine. In it 'the creature is moving fast and is more or less submerged, but appearances suggest front flippers in action'. No one seems to know what happened to these films.

*The 'Surgeon's Photograph'*
In April, 1934, the famous 'Surgeon's Photograph' was published, and after the expedition organised by Sir Edward Mountain in July, there were a number of new stills and a scrap of 16 mm. film of wakes and large ob-

75

jects moving through the water at Loch Ness, followed by the experts' unsatisfactory 'seal' conclusion.

*The 'McRae Films'*

It was a long time before any new photographs made their appearance, but in the mid-'thirties, as reported by F. W. Holiday in his book *The Great Orm of Loch Ness*, two films were reputedly taken by a Dr. McRae. After retirement from his London practice he went to live at Loch Duich, on the west coast of Scotland, and during a visit to Loch Ness early one morning he saw the Monster at no more than 100 yards range on the surface of the loch, and managed to expose several minutes of film. He could see its head, and long neck, and three humps. The eyes could be seen as slits, and two horn-like projections on the head; also a bristly mane. The head was 'bluntly conical' in profile, rather like half a rugger-ball. The creature rolled in the water during the course of the film, and a forward flipper appeared which was capable of independent movement.

In the second film Dr. McRae apparently found a similar creature lying against the shore of Loch Duich, and filmed it, too, writhing its neck over a bed of seaweed. It had a longer neck, and the mane was tufted—the substance of the mane appearing fibrous rather than hairy, and the skin tough and leathery.

Realising the significance of these two films, and concerned about the ridicule then being heaped upon the Loch Ness Monster, and those who claimed to have seen it, the good doctor decided not to show them to anyone but his closest friends. To protect them further he created a trust, so that after his death the films would not fall into the wrong hands.

So the account reads, and as Dr. McRae is now deceased it would appear unlikely that these films, if they exist, will ever be published, as the remaining trustees are bound by conditions which ensure that the films and the camera used to take them, remain safely in a bank vault.

At first sight this appears to be an incredible story. One might perhaps accept a report of *one* film, either of the Loch Ness Monster or one of its cousins in the sea, but to have filmed both types of Monster seems almost too good to be true. But if Dr. McRae lived at Loch Duich, and visited Loch Ness it *is* possible that he did see two such creatures, and that if he had had a movie-camera with him he was able to film them. Furthermore, the details of how F. W. Holiday visited one of the remaining trustees, and talked to him as described so clearly in his book, leaves one with the feeling that a hoax of such elaborate detail is unlikely, particularly as no effort had been made over the years to publicise the existence of the films.

In this case the incredible seems possible, but we have no means of obtaining proof of it. Furthermore, after so long a period the films must have deteriorated badly, which is a pity.

## The 'Taylor Film': 1938

Another short 16 mm. film was shot in 1938 by a Mr. G. E. Taylor, of Natal, who was of the opinion that he saw the Monster. It is in colour, and taken from the north shore road. It shows a straw-coloured object which changed shape, but which stayed in much the same place for some three-quarters of an hour. Opinions vary as to what it could be, but without comparison of some kind on the water, such as a boat or a scaling-marker, it is difficult to judge any object fairly.

77

## The 'Lachlan Stuart Picture': 1951

In July, 1951, a new still photograph was obtained from the south shore of Loch Ness, opposite Urquhart Bay which can be seen quite clearly in the background. It is genuine in that the water surface and ripples are quite obviously real, but the three strange humps which appear in it have been the cause of much discussion and argument as to what they could be. Lachlan Stuart (after whom the picture is now commonly named) was employed by the Forestry Commission at Loch Ness, and he and his co-witness, Mr. Taylor Hay, both saw all three humps moving together, and estimated them to be about five feet long, with about eight feet of water between each. The middle triangular-looking hump protruded about four feet out of the water, and the one in front and behind, rather less. A small head and long neck could be seen and a disturbance in the water fifteen to twenty feet behind the last hump, or so the account goes. In the picture only a dot on the surface in front could possibly be a head, so one must assume that the neck submerged just as the picture was taken. Length overall would have been fifty to sixty feet. The creature swam in to within fifty yards of the shore from about the centre of the loch, then turned away with a deal of splashing before diving below the surface, some 300 yards out.

The film and prints were processed independently, and everyone agreed that there was nothing to indicate a hoax. Mr. Stuart admitted that when the creature approached the shore both he and Mr. Hay 'moved off through the trees', although they did not actually run.

## The 'MacNab Picture': late summer, 1955

The next famous photograph to be taken, in 1955, is known today as the 'MacNab Picture'. A hand-held camera was used with six-inch telephoto lens attached.

The photographer, Mr. P. A. MacNab, did not release this remarkable picture for publication for some time afterwards, but in 1961 it was to appear in my own first book, and in *The Sunday Times*. It is a genuine picture, of that there is no doubt, and as the back of the Monster (or rather two long humps) can be seen in it moving on the surface close to Urquhart Castle tower, an idea of scale is gained. The tower stands sixty-four feet from the highest turret to the ground below.

The shape in the water is quite unlike the three almost triangular humps in the Lachlan Stuart picture, and this has caused some puzzlement. Mr. MacNab reported that the object was 'big, undulating, and moving at eight to twelve knots'. He snapped just as the creature was submerging.

## The 'Cockrell Picture': autumn, 1958

Yet another exciting still photograph was taken on Loch Ness in 1958, from a canoe. It is known today as the 'Cockrell Picture'. Mr. H. L. Cockrell had been out hunting the Monster at night in a tiny one-man canoe, and on the third successive daybreak something large approached him, and he triggered his camera. The picture is remarkably clear, and shows what appears to be a head, just breaking surface, then a water-space, finally a long low hump trailing a small wake. It is unlike any known object, and it had the effect of putting an end to Mr. Cockrell's night-time adventures on these eerie, dangerous waters! Having had long correspondence with both Mr. MacNab and Mr. Cockrell there is no doubt in my mind that they saw and photographed the Monster.

## The 'Dinsdale Film': April, 1960

My own film in 1960 produced the next photographic evidence, and a sequence of stills from it showing the

79

hump and the wake in comparison with pictures of the boat I sent out afterwards. The moving film is of course the thing to see, and when enlarged, as it has been, the hump that appears in it can be seen to be similar in shape to the middle hump in the Lachlan Stuart picture.

## The 'O'Connor Picture': May, 1960

Later in 1960, a flashlight still photograph was obtained from the north shore near Inverfarigaig, by Mr. Peter O'Connor, who had been camping on the shore with a friend in the hope of seeing the Monster. The object in the photograph shows a bulbous body, and then a neck-like protrusion breaking surface ahead of it, taken at a range of just a few yards. The vast majority of people has never seen a Monster on Loch Ness, and those who have do not always see the back in the state it was photographed by O'Connor.

I am one of the few who has. The back I saw through binoculars *before* I began to film looked exactly like the one in the O'Connor picture, so I know that it is a real picture. The most curious fact about the back that I saw through binoculars is that in the time it took me to put them down, turn to the camera, line it up and start filming—the back had altered shape! It had also started to move and submerge as shown in the film. The shape in the film is almost triangular, like the Lachlan Stuart picture.

## The 'Lowrie Picture': August, 1960

This is the wake photograph taken at a range of about forty yards from the deck of the yacht, *Finola*. It coincided with a view the Lowrie family had from on deck, of a very large unknown water animal swimming by.

80

*The 'Bureau Films': obtained 1962-72*
During this ten-year period, the Loch Ness Investigation Bureau, Limited, mounted a yearly expedition or 'investigation' manned by volunteers, and a number of long-range films was obtained of wakes and moving objects, on black and white 35 mm. film.

By far the most important of these was shot by Dick Raynor, a young volunteer cameraman, in 1967, of a wake moving on glassy-calm water opposite Dores. While this V-wash was moving slowly along, *Scott II*, the converted tug-boat, appeared conveniently in frame, whereupon the wake subsided.

The other films show disturbances and objects which are hard to evaluate, but in 1972 an interesting clip of film showed twin plumes of water proceeding across Borlum Bay at Fort Augustus, one behind the other.

*Visitors' Films and Photographs*
In recent years there has been a number of short 8 mm. movie sequences taken of objects in the water at Loch Ness. They are usually in colour, of very short duration, and of limited value as evidence. I have viewed at least three of these, and there may well be others because the publicity the Monster sometimes attracts tends to make people hide their evidence.

With the introduction of super-8 movie cameras and zoom lenses, however, there is no reason why good films cannot now be obtained by members of the public; and fears about the Press are often exaggerated.

*The 'Missed Pictures'*
Incredible though it may appear, between 1960 and 1972 no one seems to have taken a good still photograph in spite of the attempts made to do so, just two of which to my certain knowledge had the Beastie squarely in the

81

sights, only to experience a camera malfunction! In one case in 1970 seven still pictures were taken of a large Monster, followed by a little one, in broad daylight at a mere 300 yards range. The good quality 35 mm. camera and lens could have been expected to produce first-class pictures under these conditions, but by some strange misfortune the film leader tore on the wind-on sprocket, and as the lever was turned, it failed to wind on the film. The result was a completely unexposed film!

On another occasion with a Monster fully in view, the photographer found his camera lens had stuck. By the time he had freed it, the creature had submerged.

Film cameramen, too, have missed the Monster on a dozen occasions by the smallest of margins for one reason or another—giving rise to what has come to be known as the Loch Ness 'Hoodoo'.

The amount of bad luck which seems to prevent people getting photographs is extraordinary. In the old days this would, no doubt, have been attributed to the Water Kelpie legend, but today, people just shake their heads in puzzlement.

*The 'Searle Pictures': 1972*

On August 31st, 1972, Mr. Frank Searle, who is camping full-time on the shore of Loch Ness, released a still photograph of a long, two-humped object breaking surface. The photo was taken at about eighty yards, and was quite clear. *The Highland News* covered the story in the usual 'is it or isn't it?' style.

Later in the year, on November 1st, *The Daily Mirror* published three more stills by Frank Searle, taken at about 250 yards from his boat, which was some 300 yards from the shore. Two show curious-looking double-humped objects, and one showing a continuous double-humped object with what appears to be a thickish head and neck protruding out of the water to the right of it.

Inevitably, these pictures have been the cause of speculation, with those who believe them to be of the Monster, discussing features with those who think they may be of tree-trunks, or floating deer carcases, which only look like Monsters. Meanwhile, Frank Searle, who is a rugged individualist, continues his vigil hoping to gain a photograph which is beyond any doubt whatsoever.†

*The 'Rines/Edgerton' Pictures: August, 1972*

This picture, which is one of a series of 16 mm. movie-camera frames exposed underwater in Urquhart Bay by the light of a powerful strobe-flash, shows what appears to be a large flipper or paddle coinciding with a shore-based sonar-reading of a large object moving through the water. Scientifically, it is so important that it is to be discussed in Part II in the chapter on 'Results'.

† In the early months of 1973 he obtained five more photographs of a new sighting showing double-humped object and a protruding neck-like object. These pictures were displayed at his camp-site when I visited it in April with a small camera team from Nippon Television in Japan.

# Part II
# HUNTING THE MONSTER

'Voyagers and sportsmen conversant with photography are requested to take the instantaneous photograph of the animal: this alone will convince zoologists, while all other reports and pencil drawings will be received with a shrug of the shoulders.

'As these animals are very shy, it is not advisable to approach them with a steamboat.

'The *only* manner to kill one *instantly* will be by means of *explosive* balls, or by harpoons loaden with nitro-glycerine . . .'—Introductory note from *The Great Sea Serpent*, published by Dr. A. C. Oudemans, of The Hague, in 1892.

# 8

# The Monster-hunters

Monster-hunters come from all walks of life: from all age-groups, professions, jobs, nationalities and educational backgrounds. There are old Monster-hunters, and young ones, tall ones and small ones, fat ones and skinny ones, and ones with beards. There are Monster-hunters with degrees and qualifications, and those who are skilful with their hands, building houses or mining minerals. There are writers and musicians and artists amongst them; also scientists, engineers, photographers, politicians, poets, sea-captains and students.

Amongst all these people a place can always be found for new Monster-hunters who become interested in the phenomenon, and want to join in the search. Loch Ness is a very big place, and a splendid one, and there is room for everyone—in particular those with sensible ideas and honest intentions.

The Monster-hunters tend to fall into distinct categories, but in one respect they are all alike: they are inquisitive people, with open minds, who want to go and have a look for themselves. In some, this is a compelling urge, and it is in no way affected by distance. They will travel thousands of miles at their own expense just to get near the scene of action, and to take part in the work that has to be done.

Very often this involves being out in the weather for long hours, and in some cases days and nights beyond number; being half-frozen at times, and soaked at others, or burnt by the sun into blisters which would do credit to a holidaymaker on his way back from the Mediterranean!

Monster-hunters, too, are often independent to the point of being rebels, and they are sometimes referred to by society as misfits because they refuse to accept everything they are told, or live their lives out in conditions of security and—boredom. In short, they are an active, stimulating crowd of people.

From a practical viewpoint it is as well to recognise the different types of Monster-hunter, and make allowance for them within a certain category. If they are put into the wrong category they will not give of their best, and not enjoy themselves so much, and as hunting can be very hard work it is important that people enjoy themselves, too!

Rupert Gould was very much a 'loner', and as such he was typical of Monster-hunters. Today he would have been referred to as an 'independent'. This did not mean, however, that he could not work with others in a team, because he was an effective member of the Royal Navy for many years.

There are 'independents' at Loch Ness today, and they find working alone both simple and effective, but this method is but one of several, and it is not so important as teamwork.

Teamwork can be done by small groups, family groups, as often as not; or groups of friends; or even small expedition groups which get together under the leadership of some competent person, like a schoolmaster. The

88

Blackdown High School in Britain has recently put two expeditions into the field working on this basis, manned by sixth-formers.

In 1934, Sir Edward Mountain's private expedition to Loch Ness was an example of an unusual type of teamwork, which today is unheard of outside of commercial enterprise. Sir Edward *hired* men to do the watching and on a fairly big scale. Twenty men watched the loch from 9 a.m. to 6 p.m., each day stationed roughly at two-mile intervals all the way round the loch, for a period of four weeks. The observers were under the control of a Captain James Fraser, who toured the loch each day on a motorcycle, sending details on to Sir Edward at Beaufort Castle, where sightings were plotted on a map. Towards the end of the hunt, which was followed avidly by the British public through the medium of press and radio, Sir Edward and Lady Mountain, and their son Brian, spent a week at the loch themselves, watching from Urquhart Castle.

Since this first historic effort to solve the mystery there have been countless private attempts made, but it was not until July, 1960, that the first young scientists' group went into the field at Loch Ness, manned by undergraduates from Oxford and Cambridge Universities.

In 1961, the Loch Ness Investigation Bureau, Ltd., a registered charity, was formed in London by a small number of serious-minded people, and through this organisation in 1962 Monster-hunters could actually volunteer for work, and participate in long-range photographic watches.

These expeditions, starting with a two-week searchlight hunt in 1962, continued through the next ten years, growing in size and complexity with a membership reaching well above a thousand, including nationals from some fourteen different countries.

Teamwork on such a scale had never previously been

heard of at Loch Ness, but although so much effort was expended the annual 'bag' of sightings only rarely included a scrap of film to support the verbal evidence.

Curiously, the fact that no easy results could be obtained did not deter the Monster-hunters, some of whom had seen the Beast themselves and returned year after year, giving up their holidays to work independently, or with the teams of the Loch Ness Investigation—the LNI, as it came to be known.

With the passage of time, and the slow accumulation of evidence, other types of Monster-hunter began to put in an appearance—the inevitable fortune-hunters and the adventurers. These people simply added colour and excitement to the proceedings.

Some of these adventurers came to Loch Ness with tongue in cheek, but departed with a different attitude having met actual witnesses; they joined in with real enthusiasm working as hard and as long as anybody else. Even the fortune-hunters (who were few in number) would tend to alter course once they came into contact with the mainstream of enthusiasm, realising that in being selfish they missed out on nearly all the fun and comradeship.

Since the early 1930s, Loch Ness has proved a testing ground for many different people who pit their energy and initiative against the odds, and in doing so they learn to accept failure without complaint and to work out-of-doors and to co-operate with others, and above all to contribute what they can of their knowledge and ability. These generous human qualities are to be found in every true Monster-hunter, old or young, who is worthy of the title.

In recent years a new category of Monster-hunter has put in an appearance at Loch Ness known as the 'Scientific Type'. These people are generally university students working for degrees or doctorates; and there are a few mature, qualified scientists (with reputations to lose) who volunteer to assist with the fieldwork.

It is encouraging to have these specialists, and rewarding to see them pit their original minds and complicated equipment against the Ness, with its twenty-four miles of target-area, going down to nearly 1,000 feet. Very often they find that ideas which looked good on paper do not work out so well in practice, and that storms and waves make a tangle of their experiments; that equipment which works well in the laboratory, fails to work at all outside of it! These scientists, being true to their vocation, do not give in to such problems, but retire at the end of each season, muttering to themselves, and planning new experiments for the year to follow with much improved devices.

In this regard the Americans behave with typical enthusiasm and good humour, working endlessly through day and night so that in the limited time they can be over here, they make the best of their opportunity.

Equally, the young British scientists have shown a dogged perseverance. Together they make a formidable team.

From 1960 to 1973 the Monster-hunters were so active at Loch Ness that it is only possible to refer briefly to the more persistent expeditions, and the methods they adopted. Details of these adventures can be found in the Press record, and in books and articles published about them.

*Elizabeth and Torquil MacLeod:* active for two years on and around Loch Ness, in 1960 and 1961. A vehicle and boat were used to deploy experiments.

*Tim Dinsdale:* 1960–73. Eighteen private expeditions to Loch Ness; four expeditions to Loch Ness and two expeditions to Loch Morar for the LNIB; one expedition to Loch Morar in association with the LMS (Loch Morar Survey). Methods include shore-based and waterborne photography, and various experiments.

*Oxford and Cambridge joint undergraduate Expeditions:* 1960, four weeks; 1962, six weeks; Principals: Peter Baker, Bruce Ing, Mark Westwood; shore-based long-range cameras, echo-sounders, and biological experiments.

*Colonel H. G. Hasler, D.S.O., O.B.E.:* 1962, waterborne expedition to Loch Ness; fifty-six volunteers; photography, hydrophones and experiments; two months.

*Loch Ness Investigation Bureau, Ltd.:* Chairman: Norman Collins; Executive Director: David James, D.S.O., M.B.E., M.P.; Scientific Director: Dr. Roy P. Mackal (US). 1962: searchlight expedition to Loch Ness, two weeks; 1963: photographic expedition to Loch Ness, two weeks; 1964–72 inclusive: summer-long expeditions with volunteers numbered in the hundreds; shore-based photography, sonar searches, submarine searches, airborne searches, baiting, hydrophone and other experiments.

*Robert E. Love Jr.:* 1968–70: waterborne searches at Loch Ness for LNIB, sponsored by Field Enterprises Educational Corporation of Chicago; surface photography and underwater photography, sonar hydrophones and tape-sets, and experiments.

*Dan S. Taylor, Jr.:* Piloting one-man submarine *Viperfish*, 1969; one expedition to Loch Ness for LNIB, sponsored by World Book Encyclopaedia, for three months; sonar and experiments.

*Ivor Newby:* 1960–68: several private photographic and sundry expeditions to Loch Ness; 1969: five weeks waterborne on Loch Ness; surface photography; 1970: three months waterborne on Loch Ness; underwater research assisting Robert Love.

*Wing Commander K. H. Wallis:* Piloting 'Wallis 117' Autogyro; 1970 : airborne autogyro patrols, four weeks over Loch Ness, one week over Loch Morar, operating for the LNIB.

*Birmingham University: Dept. of Electronic and Electrical Engineering:* Professor D. Gordon Tucker and Hugh Braithwaite tested a digital sonar at Loch Ness in 1968 for two weeks. This equipment was again used for similar periods in 1969 with the Plessey Company and Independent Television News, who also operated a long-range Model 195 sonar. In 1970, Birmingham repeated these operations, all made in association with the LNIB.

*Black and White Scotch Expedition (United States):* 1970 : for two weeks in association with LNIB. Principals were Jack Ullrich, and Robert Lewis. Tests made with infra-red night camera.

*Academy of Applied Science (United States):* 1970 : for two weeks. Principals were Dr. Robert H. Rines and Isaac S. Blonder, Dr. Martin Klein; sidescan sonar, and other experiments; 1971 : six weeks in Loch Ness, one week in Loch Morar; underwater photography, and hydrophone/playbacks sets; 1972 : Loch Ness, six weeks; Loch Morar, one week; sonar-linked underwater and surface photography.

*Frank Searle:* 1970—onwards; full-time observation of loch from campsite near Dores; waterborne and shore-based photography.

*Nick Witchell:* 1970–71 : Private research group expeditions over a period of weeks; 1972 : five months, one-man observation of Urquhart Bay in association with LNIB; shore-based photography.

*1973 and Future Operations:* Activities are likely to develop on a continuing small private expedition, and mo-

bile group basis, as the Loch Morar Survey team has
finished its work, and the Loch Ness Investigation cannot
gain a further extension for its base camp at Achnahannet.

New scientific expeditions, or those sponsored for
commercial reasons, are likely to develop, too.

# 9

# Scientific Methods and Equipment

Perhaps one of the best aspects of the chase at Loch Ness is the very nature of the challenge it offers. It poses a major problem as experience has shown. The size of the loch, its great depth, and peat-stained water, the power and speed of the quarry, and its very rare appearances on the surface, make it an incredibly difficult target. If this was not so, it would have been 'received within the category of scientific zoology', long ago.

The history of the research effort at Loch Ness over the last ten years is fascinating, and it bristles with items of peculiar equipment which have been invented or developed to help find the Monster. Some of this equipment has produced results.

Briefly, it can be described under separate headings which show what the general purpose is, and in what field of activity it is best employed.

## Long-range Shore-based Photography
Starting with the first and most obvious research method we have photography which has been used as a tool since the very first sighting reports in 1933. To begin with, box cameras and old-fashioned plate cameras, and a few good

95

bellows cameras would have been in evidence around the loch, clutched in the hands of visitors as they scanned the water surface.

Next, as shown by Sir Edward Mountain's expedition, an attempt was made deliberately to shoot 16 mm. film with a movie-camera, and small telephoto lens.

With the improvement of cameras, lenses and film-stock it was possible to increase the range of photography, and shoot effectively on 16 mm. as shown by my own film in 1960 which recorded details at ranges up to 2,000 yards.

Later, the LNI introduced 35 mm. movie-cameras, with telescopic lenses adapted from old wartime aircraft cameras designed to photograph the ground from very high altitudes. They also used big aircraft still-cameras, which took five-inch-square negatives at regular intervals, triggered by an electric time-switch. These had a range of miles.

The best example of an ultra long-range 'rig' was built for the Loch Ness Investigation Bureau in 1964, and was soon nicknamed the 'Big Rig'. Two of these massive and splendid contrivances were placed, one on either side of the loch. The 35 mm. movie-camera in the middle was attached to a thirty-six-inch telescopic lens, and had a magazine which could hold 1,000 feet of film. Two of the big still-cameras were mounted on either side of it, aimed very slightly inwards to give a stereoscopic effect. The whole battery of cameras was attached to a tubular framework and a thick aluminium plate, which was in turn mounted on a 'Moy' head and welded steel tripod.

The watcher aimed through the cross-hairs of a tele-scope, then started all three cameras by pressing a single switch.

The Big Rigs were ingenious and could take films and photographs at enormous range, but they were also com-

Plate V—Loch Ness looking eastwards from Castle Urquhart, overlooking the deeper parts of the loch.

Plate VI—Loch Ness looking westwards towards Fort Augustus.

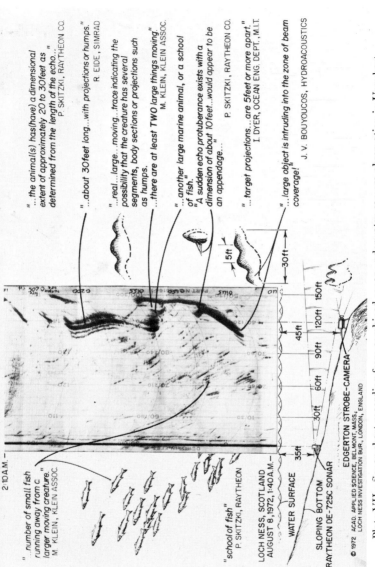

" ... the animal(s) has(have) a dimensional extent of approximately 20 to 30 feet as determined from the length of the echo ... "
P. SKITZKI, RAYTHEON CO.
R EIDE, SIMRAD

" ... about 30 feet long ... with projections or humps."
P. SKITZKI, RAYTHEON

" ... real ... large ... moving ... trace indicating the possibility that the creature has several segments, body sections or projections such as humps.
... there are at least TWO large things moving."
M. KLEIN, KLEIN ASSOC.

" ... another large marine animal, or a school of fish."
"A sudden echo protuberance exists with a dimension of about 10 feet ... would appear to be an appendage ... "
P. SKITZKI, RAYTHEON CO.

" ... target projections ... are 5 feet or more apart."
I. DYER, OCEAN ENG. DEPT., M.I.T.

" ... large object is intruding into the zone of beam coverage!"
J. V. BOUYOUCOS, HYDROACOUSTICS

2:10 A.M. —

" number of small fish running away from a larger moving creature."
M. KLEIN, KLEIN ASSOC.

"school of fish"
P. SKITZKI, RAYTHEON

LOCH NESS, SCOTLAND
AUGUST 8, 1972, 1:40 A.M. —

© 1972 ACAD. APPLIED SCIENCE, BELMONT, MASS.
LOCH NESS INVESTIGATION BUR, LONDON, ENGLAND

WATER SURFACE
SLOPING BOTTOM
RAYTHEON DE-725C SONAR
EDGERTON STROBE-CAMERA

35ft  30ft  60ft  90ft  45ft  120ft  150ft
5ft  30ft

Plate VII — Sonar chart recording from combined sonar-underwater camera observation in Urquhart Bay, 7–8th August 1972, showing 'animal(s)' with a dimensional extent of approximately 20–30 feet

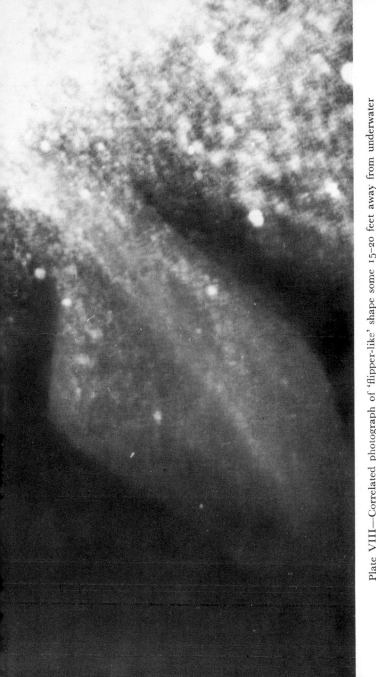

Plate VIII—Correlated photograph of 'flipper-like' shape some 15–20 feet away from underwater camera, estimated to be 6–8 feet long and 2–4 feet in width, simultaneously recorded at 01 58 hrs by sonar chart.

Plate IX—Monster-hunting by land. A 'Loch Ness Investigation' unit consisting of a 35 mm. movie camera with 36-inch telescopic lens with a range of several miles.

Plate X—Monster-hunting beneath the surface. The 2-ton submarine *Viperfish* which explored parts of Loch Ness in 1969.

Plate XI—Monster-hunting from the air. The tiny one-man Wallis autogyro with an adapted gun-camera mounted on the fuselage, which carried out aerial patrols of the loch in 1970.

plicated. When out in the weather for weeks and months at a time it was difficult to maintain them, or get replacement parts. In due course they were stripped down by the LNI, and the cameras rebuilt as single units on portable tripods. These in turn were mounted on platforms on top of panel-trucks, which came to be known as 'mobiles' —motorised camera units which were driven out each morning to places of advantage, and manned by members of the watching team.

*Air Photography*

In 1970 I was invited to run the LNIB fieldwork as 'Surface Photography Director' based on Achnahannet; and again in 1971. Having previously run teams for the LNI in 1964, and 1965 for short two-week periods, I had some idea of what was required, but things had developed in the years between.

The operation was organised by Mr. David James, M.B.E., D.S.C., M.P., founder member of the 'bureau', a Highlander by birth, and a Monster enthusiast by nature. I had first met him in 1961 when he had discussed plans for setting up the organisation which he was to mastermind thereafter as Executive Director.

In 1970, I had been thinking about air photography, or more properly air-to-water photography, because the Monster had been seen by the pilots of aircraft. Having already flown in a two-seat powered glider with this object in view, I had to decide against it because the downward view was so limited. Later, I met a certain Wing Commander K. H. Wallis who designed, built and piloted tiny one-man autogyros.

After visiting him at his country home in Norfolk, and watching a demonstration in very windy conditions, it became obvious that in this astonishing machine, the LNI would have an aerial vehicle which could mount both movie- and still-cameras, and patrol the loch from end-to-end in less than twenty minutes.

The result was a contract for Ken Wallis to fly for the Loch Ness Investigation, during the course of the summer. Altogether, five weeks of operations were carried out, and although no contact was made with the Monster the experiment was successful in terms of air-photography, with Ken Wallis obtaining beautiful panoramic still pictures and some exciting movie-films taken as the small machine chased targets on the water, and 'shot' them with an adapted gun-camera mounted on the fuselage.

Operationally, the autogyro proved a success, and as it could be towed behind a Mini-car, and fly off from any farmer's field, the patrols flown with it had more than a touch of drama, and a '007' atmosphere. Indeed, Ken Wallis had previously flown his autogyro in one of the James Bond pictures!

*Water-surface Photography*

To take pictures from the water surface implies the use of boats, or floating platforms of some kind. It also implies something which is an enemy of the photographer—instability.

Unless a boat is a big one, taking films from a tripod on board is not satisfactory, and when it is rough (as it frequently is at Loch Ness) even big boats pitch and roll in a manner which rules out a tripod.

The alternative is to hand-hold a camera, and although the human body is a marvellous automatic stabiliser, the weight of a big camera is difficult to support for any length of time, and this can lead to shaky filming. Despite these problems, however, water-surface photography is an accepted technique at Loch Ness, and although it does not offer the tremendous long-range scan of shore-based cameras, perched high up on the mountainside, there is a chance of close-up sightings—and photography, providing the cameraman has the right equipment, and does not fall overboard at the critical moment out of excitement, or fright! As far as I know, up to 1973 there have only been three photographs obtained from boats on Loch Ness, in all the years of pursuit.

*Underwater Photography*

This field is highly specialised, in which all sorts of cameras, lights, and techniques have been tried out.

The great problem at Loch Ness is the peat-stained water, which prevents photographs from being taken at more than a few feet, even with the brightest lights imaginable.

But here again experiments have been carried out in recent years using submarines, and various other bait-operated flash-camera devices, and most recently a very bright flashing light, synchronised with an underwater camera, has been tried which can take pictures every few seconds for long periods of time. This equipment has proved successful, and the results obtained in August 1972 in Loch Ness are so important that they are the subject of Chapter 11—The Rines/Edgerton 'Flipper' Picture in which a camera of this type was linked with an echo-sounder.

*Echo-sounders*

These devices, more commonly known as 'sonars' today, have been developed since the First World War when they came into use to help find enemy submarines. Since then they have been much improved and made use of in different ways: as fish-finders, underwater mapping devices, in helping locate wrecks and lost objects (like outboard motors), and even to help scientists study temperature conditions underwater.

Obviously they have an application in searching for the Monster, and have been used extensively for this with positive results.

Echo-sounders are a principal tool in any underwater search or research programme, but on their own at Loch Ness they can do no more than produce supporting evidence because they simply record the echoes from sound-pulses sent out underwater. These either come up as marks on a moving chart-paper or as dots on a TV tube, which can in turn be photographed.

Results of this kind have to be interpreted by experts who know exactly how the equipment works and what these responses indicate. A sonar does not draw a detailed outline picture and it can be fooled to some extent by false echoes, but when the results are studied by experts their comments should be taken seriously.

*Hydrophones*
Yet another tool for underwater research is the hydrophone, or listening device. This is simply a microphone, sealed into a water and pressure resistant casing which can be lowered into deep water.

If a hydrophone is connected to a tape-recorder, underwater noises can be stored and played back for analysis later on. It is surprising how many underwater creatures make noises, and once these have been identified future recorded sounds can indicate what type of animal is making them.

Thus if sounds are picked up which cannot be identified, and which do not come from an artificial source (like a telephone cable underwater), they could indicate a source which needs investigating.

*Underwater Sensing Devices*
Various other devices have been considered which would

indicate when the Monster was approaching. In theory, it would be possible to make such a device work as a trigger-mechanism for an underwater camera, but it would need to be simple and not too costly, because the danger of losing equipment underwater is a real one.

Optical, magnetic, or electronic sensing devices are possible, even mechanical contrivances. At the present time no-one has come up with a working system; but the idea remains a good one, and may have future applications.

*Baits, Lures and Stimulants*
Baits of all sorts, and concoctions have been tried at Loch Ness, to appeal to the Monster's taste and sense of smell. Sex lures and hormones have been fed gradually into the water in the hopes of luring the Monster to the surface!

Stimulating electronic waves, intended to upset the creature's balance, have been tried; sonar targets have been tried (to give the Monster the impression of a nearby shoal of fish); very loud underwater noises have been tried; underwater music has been tried; lights on and below the surface have been tried to lure the Monster closer, but all without *visible* result.

The problem with all these experiments is that without a sonar to indicate where the Monster is, no one knows what happens. When a sonar has been used, however, the story has been different.

*'Inquisitive' Experiments*
Under this heading a reference should be made to a most ingenious experiment—an attempt to excite the Monster's curiosity, by making it *talk back to itself*.

This was engineered by an American, Mr. Isaac Blonder, Chairman of the Blonder Tongue Laboratories, in New Jersey, who has built a hydrophone and tape-recorder set, which picks up incoming sounds, records them, then plays them back through an underwater speaker moments later. Thus if the Monster makes a sound nearby, it should think it is hearing another Monster talking back to it. In theory, this should make it inquisitive, excite its curiosity and make it swim over to investigate . . .

Unfortunately, this equipment worked well in the laboratory, but broke down when in service, so we do not know what its potential is.

## Computer Analysis of Habit Patterns

At the present time a computer is studying a large sample of reports to see if any odd habit pattern can be isolated. If such proves to be the case it may be possible to watch at certain places, or under certain conditions, with a better-than-average chance of success.

## Biopsy Darts and Tissue Samples

The idea that a small sample of Nessie's skin would be useful to geneticists is an obvious one, and if this could be obtained without harming the creature, there is no reason why it should not be. The problem remains of how to get it.

Various ideas have been tested, including cross-bows as projectors—but they are complicated, and at close range it is doubtful whether anyone would have the time or courage to use one!

There are alternative schemes, which might yield results, but on a hit-and-miss basis. The problem to date has been to get within half-a-mile of the Monster.

For this reason, too, radio-transmitter darts, or hypo-tranquillising darts (which could be useful in theory), cannot be put into practice, and at Loch Ness there is very little point in doing anything which is not practical.

## Underwater Vehicles

As experience has already shown, submarines and submersibles in Loch Ness suffer from being almost blind due to the stained water; and as research vehicles they are often extremely slow and have no chance at all of keeping up with the Monster.

However, Dan Taylor's little yellow submarine *Viperfish* may have come very close to the Monster in 1969. The two-ton craft was resting on the bottom 130 feet down in Urquart Bay, when it was swirled round through 180 degrees, and the bottom silt churned up. No ordinary fish could have done that. Unfortunately, he did not have his search sonar on at the time, but a bigger submarine called *Pisces* did get a 'blip' on sonar 470 feet down in the Bay, later in the summer.

High-speed submarines, with search equipment of the type used by the Royal Navy might well be able to chase the Monster, and track it with sonar, but until Monster-hunting is made respectable, there is no chance of this happening.

In the future, no doubt, submarines will play an important part in the research yet to be done.

## Trapping Equipment

As the Monsters exist it must be possible to catch one, a small one anyway, but no one has yet come up with a means of doing this. Some thought has been given to the matter, however, and there are practical methods which could probably isolate a specimen without harming it, which is very important. No one has the right to destroy one of these astonishing animals.

10

# Results

With so much equipment in use and so much voluntary effort being expended in search of the Monster, it is fair to ask about results. Do they amount to anything scientifically? And, in terms of useful human employment, is the effort worthwhile?

To both these questions we can answer in the affirmative. For once we can say 'yes', without ifs-and-buts, and without having to suggest alternatives, or probabilities in the answer. It is simply 'Yes'.

Scientifically, there is now some good evidence, and in the human sector, we can point to encouraging results : years of voluntary, intelligent work done by numbers of different people prepared to give up their time to field-work and research, without expecting a reward, beyond a sense of satisfaction and the pure enjoyment of doing something exciting and worthwhile. These are results !

But in science it is necessary to be able to measure results, and to provide a permanent record of them. Verbal testimony in law is acceptable as evidence, and in the past enough of it was sufficient to hang a man, but in science it is different. No matter how many people claim to have seen the Monster unless they are able to photograph it, or record its passage on a graph or TV tube, science will do no more than consider these reports as 'interesting'. They do not constitute proof.

If, however, records can be made which are real and accurate, science should in theory take note of them, and equally, take action.

Results so far obtained are subject to interpretation. The fact that a film has been shot of a large moving object at a distance does not prove what the object is. It may be man-made, the product of a hoax; or some peculiar natural object; or some peculiar natural effect. On the other hand it may be a film of the Loch Ness Monster. The interpretation of such a film is a matter of measurements, comparisons, and common-sense deductions.

Real evidence so far obtained comes under the headings 'Sonar Results' and 'Photographic Results'. No one at the present time has found any bodily remains at Loch Ness, or secured a tissue sample that we know about.

*'Sonar Results'*
The first organised search with an echo-sounder was made in 1960, by the Oxford and Cambridge Expedition. The work done was reported in *The Scotsman* on the 12th, 13th and 14th of September, by Richard Arnold and Peter F. Baker—now Dr. Peter Baker. Contacts were made and recorded from large moving and diving objects underwater, which did not appear to be fish.

In 1962, the second expedition worked with more advanced equipment: results included 'a strong echo from an unidentified object off Urquhart Castle on July 20th'. This report by Peter Baker and Mark Westwood appeared in *The Observer* on August 26th. An echo-chart was published showing a long, dense recording, in comparison with that from a 25 ft. yacht at 300 yards which was much smaller. During sixty hours of operation two strong echoes were recorded. In conclusion, the authors said . . . 'After two expeditions to Loch Ness we cannot say with conviction that the Loch Ness Monster does not exist. Indeed, the small pieces of evidence we have all suggest that there is an unusual animal in the loch. . . .'

The next sonar results were obtained in 1968 when a team from Birmingham University tried out a new type of digital sonar, working with the LNIB from Urquhart Bay. Again, echoes were obtained from moving and diving objects underwater which did not appear to be fish. These results were reported in *The New Scientist*, on 19th December, 1968, and in the Bureau's Annual Report for that year. Professor D. Gordon Tucker, and Hugh Braithwaite, of the Department of Electronic and Electrical Engineering, worked the equipment, and prepared the report. In it, the comment is made . . . 'Since the objects A and C are clearly comprised of animals, is it possible they could be fish? The high rate of ascent and descent makes it seem very unlikely, and fishery biologists we have consulted cannot suggest what fish they might be . . .'

In 1969, Robert E. Love, Jr., continued the search from a boat fitted with a Honeywell Scanner II sonar, covering more than 160 miles, in forty-five hours' patrolling. This equipment was monitored by movie-cameras which took pictures of the sonar screen and the 'blips' or echo responses coming up on it. Some 20,000 frames were exposed and several 'targets' were recorded. One of these was tracked for 2 minutes 19 seconds as it followed a looping path underwater before speeding up to escape from the sonar beam. This is reported in intriguing detail by Bob Love in the 1969 LNIB Annual Report, complete with diagrams and photographs.

In 1970, Dr. Robert H. Rines, and Dr. Martin Klein of the Academy of Applied Science team from Belmont,

Massachusetts, tried out yet another type of sonar. This was a side-scan sonar designed by Dr. Klein who operated it. It was a short-range high definition sonar, and when set up in Urquhart Bay 'intruders' were seen to be moving through the sound-beam underwater. They came up as marks on a big sepia-coloured chart.

Later, the sonar 'fish' was trailed from *Water Horse*, a small power-boat the LNIB had chartered, further down the loch in very deep water. I skippered her for three days, and watched with fascination as large blips appeared on the chart. They were immensely bigger than the dots that indicated salmon and trout.

In due course, the Academy, of which Bob Rines was President, issued a report:

'In summary, our brief side-scan sonar tests in Loch Ness in 1970 produced three important discoveries:
1. There are large moving objects in the loch.
2. There is abundant fishlife in the loch which could support a large creature.
3. There are large ridges in the steep walls of the loch which could conceivably harbour large creatures.'

In 1971, Dr. Rines returned with a very special type of underwater flashing device and movie-camera which worked together for up to twenty-four hours, taking single frames every few seconds. In the spring he had invited me over to the United States to give talks about Loch Ness, and Professor Harold Edgerton from M.I.T. (Massachusetts Institute of Technology) had attended one of them. He was the world's leading authority on strobe-light underwater photography, and afterwards invited us round to his laboratory to show us this equipment. Later he built a strobe-camera set for the Academy to use.

Beyond testing this in Loch Ness and Loch Morar in 1971, no Monster photographs were obtained until August, 1972, when the device was linked with a sonar. These are the results described separately in Chapter 11.

*'Photographic Results'*
'Photographic results' which have been studied by competent, independent experts and made the subject of reports, are few in number. David James at the LNIB deserves full credit, however, for gaining the help of the R.A.F. to study films through the Joint Air Reconnaissance Intelligence Centre. 'JARIC', as it is known by Monster-hunters today, has done a unique job of interpretation based on measurement as described by David James in his Loch Ness Investigation Annual Report for 1966 . . .

'Shortly after my return from the U.S., there was a significant development. I had become much impressed by the R.A.F. (JARIC) reports on film submitted by us for interpretation; and, with his permission, sent them Tim Dinsdale's 1960 film . . . In February there arrived a weighty and closely argued case, to show that the object was almost certainly animate, 12–16 ft. long, 3 ft. high, nearly 6 ft. in beam, and travelling at ten knots. The ability of photographic interpreters to argue to less than an inch at 1,500 yards, strengthened our determination to attempt conclusive head-and-neck photography, and our thanks are due to Lord Shakleton, Minister of State for Defence (Air), and his Intelligence Staff, for their help . . .'

This report, which ran to some 2,000 words had a profound effect at the time, and has been printed as a pamphlet since. It is a Crown Copyright document.

In 1967, too, Dick Raynor shot his clear sequence of film off Dores, and again JARIC reported. They said an object broke surface where the wake commenced, measuring about seven feet in length.

The other scraps of long-range film have also been examined, but they are so brief, and the objects so far away, that it is hard to interpret them.

In consequence, the Monster-hunters have yet to achieve their main objective: good, clear, movie-film of Nessie taken at close range.

# 11

# The Rines/Edgerton 'Flipper' Picture

In August, 1972, after a brief visit to Loch Morar, Dr. Robert Rines returned again to Loch Ness, but on this occasion armed with a compact Raytheon sonar, to work in conjunction with the Edgerton underwater strobe electronic flash-camera, which had been tested out the year before.

He set up 'shop' in Urquhart Bay in a particular spot where the great trenches in the bottom of the bay seemed to provide the best chance of intercepting the Monster. The year before, the bottom had been criss-crossed with boats, and mapped from the echo-charts obtained. His work had shown what a very strange place the Bay was underwater, and to demonstrate this Bob Rines had prepared a model which was put on show, and photographs of which appeared in the LNI's information centre.

Two boats were used, beneath each of which was an item of equipment—the sonar, and the strobe-camera.

On the 29th October, 1972, the LNIB issued a confidential newsletter to its members, stating that . . .

'On the night of August 7–8th, the Academy of Applied Science—Loch Ness Investigation Bureau team, led by Dr. Robert H. Rines, was operating an underwater camera and sonar in Urquhart Bay, Loch Ness. The sonar (a Raytheon Explorer III model) was operated from the LNIB research vessel *Narwhal* which was moored approximately 60 yards from the shore near Temple Pier while the underwater stroboscopic camera was suspended beneath the cabin cruiser *Nan*, chartered for use in this series of experiments with the help of Commander Bodie, of Knockie Lodge. *Nan* was moored approximately 100 yards from shore and about 40 yards further out than *Narwhal*. The transducer [sonar transmitter] was aligned so that any object(s) coming into camera range would be detected by the sonar. During the night several large objects were recorded on the sonar chart, and luckily these were subsequently found to have been photographed. . . .

'Before even seeing any of the photographs, the Raytheon Company stated : ". . . it may be determined from the record at 0105 hours, 0117 hours, and 0157 hours that the animal(s) has (have) a dimensional extent of approximately 20–30 feet as determined from the length of the echo returns . . . The record shows extended echo returns beginning at 0143 hours with the object(s) moving away from the transducer. A sudden echo protuberance exists with the dimension of about 10 feet, and shows for less than a minute. It appears to be correlated with the extended echo return, moving at the same speed and would appear to be an appendage brought into reflective aspect for a short period of time."

'At the times mentioned above photographs were obtained of a long appendage. On board *Narwhal* at the time were LNI members Peter Davies, Hilary Ross and David Wiseman. Soon after the first large traces appeared, a quartz-iodide searchlight was played on the surface of the water along the line of the sonar beam. While the light was on, this object seemed to come towards the transducer for a short distance and when it was switched off the object moved away. This occurred several times . . .'

Shortly after this event Bob Rines flew down from Scotland, and as I had come south myself for a few days between expeditions, I met him at the airport. He showed me the echo-graph and we discussed the possibilities. Clearly, if there was anything on the film, it could prove to be of tremendous importance, because no one had previously been able to get underwater pictures of the Monster, and no one had put a camera underwater within a sonar-beam. The two pieces of separate equipment would prove each other's results! This arrangement could put the evidence beyond doubt scientifically.

Back in the U.S., the film-cassette was delivered to Eastman Kodak to be processed under control. When examined, several frames of the colour film had something in them which coincided with the sonar recordings. The images were faint and difficult to interpret through the murk of the Loch Ness water, but the objects were at extreme camera-range under these conditions about fifteen to twenty feet away.

But they *did* exist, and in one picture a quite definite flipper-like shape could be seen. Taken in sequence, at 1.48 a.m. the camera recorded nothing but water. Thirty seconds later an object entered the strobe-beam at extreme photo-range. Fifteen seconds later a structural appendage resembling a 'flipper' appeared, optically measured as about '6 to 8 feet' with a maximum width of '2 to 4' feet. Fifteen seconds later a tail-like structure at least '8 feet long' appeared, at about the same time as the sonar chart recorded a '10 foot appendage'. Fifteen seconds later there was clear water again. The intruder had gone.

In order to improve these pictures, they were submitted for processing by a computer, which is able to analyse what really is in a picture, and then improve the picture quality. The same process has been used in America for improving pictures from space, of the Moon and Mars, with clear results.

The result in the case of the 'flipper-picture' was most dramatic, revealing a great diamond-spade-shaped limb which, as the optical measurements had shown, was of huge proportions: six to eight feet long and from two to four feet in width.

The indisputable fact of this picture is just as important as the size and shape of the object shown in it; and as all the famous milestones in photography at Loch Ness have in the past carried the names of those who recorded them we should in future refer to this as the Rines/Edgerton picture, in salute to the two men whose combined talents made it possible: Professor Harold Edgerton at the Massachusetts Institute of Technology, and Dr. Robert Rines, President of the Academy of Applied Science. The LNI, too, deserves a well-earned round of applause for their support during the course of these experiments, and the young men and women on the team who were at their monitoring posts at two o'clock in the morning. This was team-work at its best.

The sonar and photo-analysts, who have studied these results, include some of the world's best-known experts and institutions who estimated sizes and distances from the sonar chart and photographs; and in defence of the mechanical-expert, the electronic genius which brought out the detail in the picture—the computer, it is very interesting to note that it does *not* make mistakes.

At the time of a second lecture tour in America at the invitation of the Academy in the spring of 1972, I visited California. I left behind my precious original 1960 film for the computer to study also, with the result that it has been shown to contain indications of a second and possibly a third hump, or tail, following the first one. If one knows precisely when to look in the film, the second hump can be seen following in the wake of the one ahead. This came as an exciting moment for me, because I had never spotted it before, and it took the computer to point it out. This also proved that combining the efforts of men and machines is the right technique at Loch Ness.

# 12

# Do's and Don'ts of Monster-hunting

In this modern era of good cameras and inexpensive tele-photo lenses, an opportunity exists for any Monster-hunter to obtain clear pictures of a sighting.

Loch Ness has a sixty-mile perimeter, and some marvellous scenery, and natural effects. It is a paradise for the naturalist, with its wild birds, and roaming herds of deer; its fishing and climbing for the sportsman, are second to none.

But above all, it contains one of the world's greatest natural mysteries and marvels . . . the Loch Ness Monsters. It cannot be so very long now before they become accepted as a fact in Britain, with consequent protection, and in due course, study, through perhaps an internationally founded research centre at the lochside.

The very nature and unique importance of this coming discovery will make it once again a target for the Press, for radio and television, and world attention as a result. When this happens, and it is beginning to happen now, there will be a danger of the natural beauties being spoiled or swamped by multitudes of visitors who leave a trail of picnic debris round the loch.

This need not happen, and if people behave with

intelligence, there is room and opportunity for them to enjoy the place and the scenery, and to look out for the Monster themselves.

Young people in particular may want to join in the hunt, and to experience the tingle of excitement as they gaze out over the enchanted waters of the loch. But if they are to do this usefully and safely, it is best done from the higher shoreline with a tripod and long-lens camera.

The waters of the Ness are very, very cold—and at times unbelievably rough. To fall out of a canoe, or other small craft, can mean a quick death from exposure if no other boat is close. It is necessary to get a human body out of the water quickly, to avoid the heat-loss that brings unconsciousness in half-an-hour or less. There are few boats, and the loch surface covers thirteen thousand acres. It is no place to fool about.

Better by far to adopt the mobile role ashore, with a vehicle which can provide shelter when needed, a place to sleep and eat, and a platform for a camera. The problem of supply on expeditions is vitally important, and at Loch Ness a vehicle is essential. It also enables the Monster-hunter to move from place to place, to circuit the loch during the term of his expedition, and thus avoid boredom; and get to see the place in all its majestic splendour of light and shade, and mist upon the water.

Should a new Monster-hunter be lucky, and he would need to be very lucky, there is always a real chance of a Monster photograph. Once taken, a photograph, or indeed a film, needs some form of comparison on the water. To obtain this, seek the help of a member of the LNI, should they be in evidence or on mobile patrol around the loch. They will fix up a boat to move down loch and provide a scaling marker.

Monster-hunting can be fun, but it requires a deal of concentration. It is not a game, but those who are genuinely interested in the search can contribute to it by watching, too. If they have a still-camera with telephoto lens, they have a sporting chance of gaining photographic evidence, and this should be made available as soon as possible for analysis. No picture is of much value unless it can be viewed by those who are able to measure it, and assess its contents zoologically. The copyright of any picture remains the property of the photographer unless sold to someone else. It is best not to sell it in my view, because it is important that pictures are made available to researchers, on a non-commercial basis.

Finally, the question of good sense and bodily self-protection arises. No experienced Monster-hunter will go into the field without clothing designed to protect him, or her, from the wind and cold, the rain, and equally the sun. For the latter a broad-rimmed hat is essential, and dark glasses, too. Surprisingly, it is quite possible to get sunstroke at Loch Ness if unprotected in a heatwave.

Rain-protection clothing should be of the non-porous type, and of rain-shedding design. It is pointless having trousers tucked into socks and shoes which will simply fill with water when it rains for hours and days as it sometimes does! The cold wind, too, at dawn can paralyse, so to be sure to have a truly wind-proof jacket and over-trousers. A woollen cap of the type that yachtsmen use is also an essential, and depending on the time of year, a woollen scarf and gloves. There is no point in being knocked out by the weather!

In the warmer summer months, from June through to the latter part of August, make absolutely certain that you carry an effective insect repellent cream, and be prepared to use it. There are minute monsters at the loch called MIDGES. These pin-head-sized insects bite like white-hot needles, and can wreck an expedition. They hatch in clouds, in warm, moist conditions.

All expeditions need to be planned carefully. It is pointless arriving at Loch Ness unprepared, but if a few definite plans are made in advance, and the right attitude adopted towards problems which may develop unexpectedly, the rewards can be great. The beauty of Loch Ness, and the undercurrents of excitement which flow around it create an atmosphere which no Monster-hunter can easily forget.

And for those who do not have time for long expeditions, or the money to buy special equipment, Loch Ness can still prove to be an exciting place to visit. To circuit the loch by road can be a breathtaking experience, and if the visibility is good there is always a chance of seeing a Monster-wake, or even one of these strange animals moving on the surface.

Anyone of any age can be a useful observer, and enjoy the thrill of gazing out over the huge expanse of water. Artificial aids to vision, like a pair of binoculars, are of course a help, but as these are expensive a small telescope is a good alternative—and at half the price. If a telescope is used, the front end of it should be rested on something solid like a wall, or the top of a car roof.

If a sighting occurs, observations should be written down as soon as possible afterwards, and signed by witnesses. If possible, sketches should be drawn, with as much detail included as memory permits. Estimates of distance and size are often inaccurate, but some attempt should be made to include both.

If any member of the group has a tape-recorder, or can borrow one, witnesses should tape an account of their sighting as naturally and expressively as they can. This is probably the most convincing way of recording evidence other than on film.

Only by patient effort can we collect new evidence at Loch Ness, and learn more about the colony of great unknown animals which inhabits the dark and mysterious depths. Only by presenting this evidence intelligently can we gain for them a national recognition, and the protection and study which will follow.

If we do this then we will also make a very special place for them 'within the category of Scientific Zoology'—the record of our natural heritage within these historic Islands of Great Britain.

## Morag, the Monster of Loch Morar

# Supplement

## Morag, the Monster of Loch Morar

Loch Morar, just off the west Highland shoreline, is reputedly the deepest lake in Britain, but with the new depths discovered by the submarine *Pisces*, in Loch Ness in 1969, it almost lost the title; there being only some forty-two feet difference between the two.

Morar is eleven miles in length, has a depth of 1,017 feet, crystal-clear water, and a beauty which is almost unreal. The mountains are softer than at Loch Ness, with a mossy velvet texture, but at the head of the loch they rise in a towering cleft to nearly 4,000 feet. It is a remote, silent place, with no roads around it, and very few people. The western tip is accessible to motorists, and there are a few boats at this, the shallow end. The remainder of the loch, with its islands and crystalline beaches, and its great depths, is lonely, and untouched. It is also privately owned, and thus protected. It is a place of the spirit.

Loch Morar, too, has for long carried a mysterious tradition—the legend of its own particular Monster, as told by the 'Old People' and surrounded with an aura of dread; for when the *Mhorag* was seen it was considered an omen of death for a member of the Gillies clan.

Constance Whyte in her book *More Than a Legend*,

refers to Loch Morar, and included actual reports of the Monster; but it was not until July, 1972, that it became the focus of a new book entirely devoted to the research effort made by the Loch Morar Survey team in 1970 and 1971. In this, Elizabeth Montgomery Campbell and Dr. David Solomon combined to present the legendary evidence and scientific facts, in a manner which is both clear and readable.

Since publication of *The Search for Morag* by Tom Stacey, Ltd., the LMS returned to Morar for a third expedition in 1972, and from out of this adventure a new eye-witness report was recorded by 'Liz' Montgomery Campbell herself. And as I had the good fortune to spend two weeks with the expedition, she has kindly consented to write down her experience for this book.

As a brief introduction, however, it is important to say that at Loch Morar the background history and recent sighting evidence points to a colony of unknown animals similar to those reported in Loch Ness. Furthermore, Loch Morar, too, was recently an arm of the sea. It, too, has a big fish population, and the scientific study done by the Survey team has shown that the loch is not a sterile body of water, but an actively productive one in terms of food-chain. This means it could provide enough food for a colony of predators.

The account reads :

'*July 19th, 1972—Mrs. E. Montgomery Campbell—*
*Sighting at Loch Morar*

'Ever since our arrival at Morar five days earlier the weather had been so hot that we almost wished it would cool down and make working easier—or, at least, we would have wished this if we had not known that this was classic "sighting" weather.

'Tuesday, July 19th, was once more hot and sunny, and when I went on camera watch at about 9.45 am there was not a breath of wind and the surface of the loch was flat calm. Our camera, a 16 mm. Bolex, was set up on a small headland beside White Beach where we had pitched camp; to the east was a small bay known locally as Caravan Bay because two or three caravans were permanently parked there.

'By ten o'clock a light breeze was beginning to get up and was ruffling the surface over to the west by the islands, where two of our boats were being used to carry out sonar experiments. There were no other boats or people to be seen and I felt very solitary as I scanned the loch surface for any unusual object.

'At seven minutes past ten I suddenly became aware of a long, thin, black object lying on the surface of the water just off a small reef of rocks jutting out into the water, east of Caravan Bay. The object was stationary and remained so for such a long time that I began to wonder if it was the top of some more rocks that I hadn't previously noticed—even though I was sure that by now, I *would* have noticed them. I also noticed a long white streak trailing back from the object, the sort of streak you sometimes get after a powerboat has gone by. The object itself was only a few inches above the water, and about six or seven feet long. Detailed examination was difficult as I was looking in the direction of the sun.

'Twenty minutes later I saw that the object had vanished. The wind coming from the west had now reached Caravan Bay and the surface was rippled. Could it have been a low reef of rocks that only showed in still water? I made a note in the log book to check next time there was a flat calm.

'And then, about ten minutes later, I saw what looked like the same long thin black object, only this time farther away. Looking through binoculars I saw that it was beginning to move; it was now a definite low-lying hump, about six feet across and not more than eighteen inches high, moving diagonally round the headland at about one or two knots. Although it went so slowly there was a distinct low, white wash. Because of the position of the sun I couldn't see its colour, but it looked dark, with a definite shine on top.

'I thought of all the things it might have been—a boat, a floating log, a diving bird, an otter—all these flashed through my mind in turn. But it wasn't. It was a hump, moving and making a wash. I knew at last that the stories about the Loch Morar sightings were based on truth.

'I wish this story had a happy ending—but by the time I knew for sure that this was a genuine sighting, I also knew that in a very few seconds the hump would be out of sight behind the next headland, and that even if I could have filmed it against the sun, there wasn't time. All I could do was go on looking, so that at least I could write all the details down straight away and know that they would be as accurate as possible.

'The whole sighting lasted between twelve and fifteen seconds, and then the hump had gone out of sight. I shouted a message to one of the Survey members, and Tim in his boat *Hunter* was on the spot a few minutes later together with one Survey member in our third boat, but they saw nothing at all that could have caused the sighting.

'Just as I finished writing the details down a man came up to me. "Did you have any boats out about two o'clock this morning?" he asked me. "No," I said, "they were all back by midnight. Why?"

'He nodded. "Just wanted to make sure. You see, me and my mate were out fishing in Caravan Bay last night. The water was like a sheet of glass. Yet about 1.30 a.m.

our boat was rocked by bow waves, as though a big boat had gone past. We didn't see anything and there wasn't any sound of an engine. It happened again about two, and again at two-thirty. What's more, we didn't get any fish at all, though the night before we'd been pulling them out one after the other."

' "I thought you might like to know." '

In closing this account I can do no better than quote a verse from an old Scottish lay, published by the authors of *The Search for Morag* on the title page.

In just four lines it captures the atmosphere, the sense of awful mystery which affects those who probe into the depths of Loch Morar:

'Morag, Harbinger of Death,
          Giant swimmer in deep-green Morar,
              The loch that has no bottom . . .
        There it is that Morag the monster lives.'

# STAY ON

Here are details of other exciting TARGET titles. If you cannot obtain these books from your local bookshop, or newsagent, write to the address below listing the titles you would like and enclosing cheque or postal order—*not* currency—including 5p per book to cover postage and packing. Postage is free for orders in excess of three titles.

TARGET BOOKS,
Universal-Tandem Publishing Co.,
14 Gloucester Road,
London SW7 4RD

## INVESTIGATING UFOs                                    25p
### Larry Kettelkamp
0 426 10006 9                                  **A Target Mystery**
The full, dramatic story of unidentified flying objects or "Flying Saucers" as they are commonly called. Visitors from other planets? Optical illusions? Or practical jokes? With the help of INVESTIGATING UFOs you can decide for yourself and even join one of the 20 or more UFO clubs in the United Kingdom. *Fully illustrated with photographs and drawings.*

## FISHING
**J. H. Elliott**
25p

0 426 10145 6

Fishing, or angling, is the most popular outdoor hobby for all ages. This book advises on the choice of equipment; baits; fishes, and how to catch them; do's and don'ts; and how to enjoy your angling. For the beginner and partially experienced alike. *Illustrated*.

## PETER PIPPIN'S SECOND BOOK OF PUZZLES
25p

0 426 10102 2

Thousands of young people all over the country tackle Peter Pippin's puzzles every week in their local paper. Here is another collection to baffle and entertain the whole family!

## WINGS OF GLORY
**Graeme Cook**
30p

0 426 10014 x
**Target True-life Adventure**

Read how the dread-inspiring *Zeppelin* airships of World War I were destroyed; how the 'indestructible' "Red Baron", all-time ace of German fighter-pilots, met his end; how Britain won her greatest battle; how the *Kamikaze* suicide-pilots nearly turned the tide of war in the Pacific; how the "Dambusters" flooded Hitler's industrial Ruhr with millions of gallons of water; and other stories of skill and courage in the skies! *Illustrated*.

and coming in September, 1973
## NONE BUT THE VALIANT
Stories of war at sea
**Graeme Cook**

## DOCTOR WHO
**David Whitaker**
25p

(based on the famous BBC television series)

0 426 10110 3
**A Target Adventure**

DOCTOR WHO's first exciting adventure with the Daleks! Ian Chesterton and Barbara Wright travel with the mysterious DOCTOR WHO, and his grand-daughter Susan, to the planet of Skaro in the space-time machine, *Tardis*. There they strive to save the peace-loving Thals from the evil intentions of the hideous Daleks. Can they succeed? And what is more important, will they ever again see their native Earth? *Illustrated*.

## DOCTOR WHO AND THE ZARBI 25p
**Bill Strutton**

0 426 10129 4  **A Target Adventure**

DOCTOR WHO lands his space-time machine *Tardis* on the cold, craggy planet of Vortis. The Doctor and his companions, Ian and Vicki, are soon captured by the Zarbi, huge ant-like creatures with metallic bodies and pincer claws; meanwhile Barbara falls into the hands of the friendly Menoptera who have come to rid Vortis of the malevolent power of the Zarbi.... *Illustrated.*

## DOCTOR WHO AND THE CRUSADERS 25p
**David Whitaker**

0 426 10137 5  **A Target Adventure**

Back on Earth again, *Tardis* lands DOCTOR WHO and his friends into the midst of the harsh, cruel world of the twelfth-century Crusades. Soon the adventurers are embroiled in the conflict between Richard the Lionheart and the Sultan Saladin, ruler of the warlike Saracens. . . . *Illustrated.*

## THE NIGHTMARE RALLY 25p
**Pierre Castex**

0 426 10081 6  **A Target Adventure**

The exciting story on which Walt Disney based their film— *Diamonds on Wheels*. Robert, an apprentice garage-mechanic, creates *Ferblantine* from the crashed remains of a Renault Dauphine and enters her for the 6th Brie Car Rally. But there is more to *Ferblantine* than Robert suspects, and both he and his friend Serge become involved in a truly nightmare rally with ruthless diamond smugglers on their tail . . . A "must" for all car-lovers.

## THE LONER 25p
**Ester Wier**

0 426 10022 0  **A Target Adventure**

"You haven't got it, boy. You've proved that. I think you picked the wrong name. You'll never make a shepherd." But David, a stray, or 'loner', who had chosen his name at random from Boss's Bible, proves her wrong in a breathtaking encounter with a huge, grizzly bear.... *Illustrated.*

If you enjoyed this book and would like to have information sent you about other TARGET titles, write to the address below.

*You will also receive:*

## A FREE TARGET BADGE!

Based on the TARGET BOOKS symbol—see front cover of this book—this attractive three-colour badge, pinned to your blazer-lapel, or jumper, will excite the interest and comment of all your friends!

*and you will be further entitled to:*

## FREE ENTRY INTO THE TARGET DRAW!

All you have to do is cut off the coupon beneath, write on it your name and address *in block capitals*, and pin it to your letter. You will be advised of your lucky draw number. Twice a year, in June and December, numbers will be drawn 'from the hat' and the winner will receive a complete year's set of TARGET books.

Write to: TARGET BOOKS,
Universal-Tandem Publishing Co.,
14 Gloucester Road,
London SW7 4RD

———————————————— cut here ————————————————

Full name.........................................................................

Address..........................................................................

........................................................................................

.............................. County........................................

Age...............................